PRAISE FOR
THE MAKING OF A MYSTIC

"One of my mentors used to say, 'What is most personal to you is most universal to me.' That's how I felt when I read Kevin Sweeney's new book. By telling the story of his spiritual journey, Kevin sparked my own spiritual curiosity and hunger. You may never have considered yourself a mystic, but in these pages, you'll find resonance with some of your own deepest hopes, longings, and intuitions."

Brian D. McLaren
Author of *Do I Stay Christian?*

"The paths that lead us to the Holy One are many. Those who choose to continue the search for an intimate connection with the Divine, no matter where they are led, are few. Kevin Sweeney surrendered to a journey that makes it possible to seek both truth and wisdom, while honoring his life choices as a husband, father, pastor, and friend. If you are intrigued by the idea of apprenticing with one who is becoming a mystic, Kevin is your guide. As for me, I'm all in!"

Suzanne Stabile
Author of *The Path Between Us* and *The Journey Toward Wholeness*

"The word 'mystic' is bandied about by so many spiritualists these days, it's hard to know what it means anymore. That's why I'm grateful for Kevin Sweeney, a seasoned spiritual guide who has done the work on the topics of mysticism, both in theory and in practice. Sweeney shows us the sacredness of suffering, silence, and solitude. *The Making of a Mystic* offers a panoramic field guide for anyone seeking to move beyond the bounds of popular faith constructs and into a more reflective, contemplative spirituality."

Jonathan Merritt
Contributing writer for *The Atlantic* and
author of *Learning to Speak God from Scratch*

"Kevin Sweeney has not been working on growing a popular public platform. Instead, he has cultivated the inner peace and joy of a mystic yielding himself to God and embracing the uncontrollable world and reality we navigate every day. Thankfully, in *The Making of a Mystic*, Sweeney has gifted us all with a guided journey that leads all the way from the cosmos to our interior lives. Read this vital book!"

Drew G. I. Hart, Ph.D.
Author of *Who Will Be A Witness?: Igniting Activism for God's Justice, Love, and Deliverance* and Co-host of Inverse Podcast

"When one thinks of a 'mystic', we tend to think of gurus tucked away in mountain monasteries who spend their day meditating in search of transcendent experiences. While that may be one way to experience the mystical, Kevin Sweeney's book *The Making of a Mystic* reveals a more accessible path for the rest of us. Through captivating stories from his own journey and practical wisdom, Sweeney walks the reader on a path towards profound spiritual depth and a renewed sense of joy and awe at life. This is a book for seekers, wanderers, and skeptics who are longing for a travel companion as they follow the inner nudging in their Spirit to explore the depths of meaning and reality. Every page will challenge you, inspire you, and absolutely enthrall you—so buckle up and prepare to be transformed."

Brandan Robertson
Author of *Filled to Be Emptied:*
The Path of Liberation for Privileged People

"The foundations of Spirituality under our feet seem to be crumbling. Deconstruction is all around us. We need guidance in this great unknown. *The Making of a Mystic* just might be the sage and sacred path forward. No, the path forward Sweeney lays out is not doubling down on doctrines or dogma. Rather it's an invitation to let go, a contemplative journey that will breathe air back into disillusioned faith. Part memoir, part confessional conversation with poetic rhyme, you will find an old but new path in these pages. Being a mystic is not just for old dead guys, Kevin Sweeney has unlocked it for everybody!"

Dan White Jr.
Author of *Love Over Fear* and Co-founder of The Kineo Center

"*The Making of a Mystic* is a profoundly timely message at a critical time in the evolving story of faith, spirituality, and Christianity. Kevin writes from a place of personal knowing and embodiment. He will simultaneously make you laugh, challenge you to greater depths and invite you to more and more freedom. If you are looking for next steps on your spiritual journey into the life of actually knowing God and experiencing Spirit—the path of the mystic—then this book is for you. Read this book to have your mind and heart expanded and have a really good time along the way. We couldn't recommend it highly enough."

Phil and Jen Wood
Hosts of "The Phil and Jen Podcast" and
co-founders of Redemption Church

"Before I went to graduate school, I thought 'a mystic' was something similar to a spiritual wizard … like a faithful Gandalf. Mystics were larger than life, someone beyond comprehension and certainly impossible to imitate. It was in seminary that I encountered the writings of some of my favorite mystics and my notion of what mysticism changed. I haven't had such a profound new understanding of mysticism until now. Kevin Sweeney's book has once again brought mysticism to a level of comprehension and curiosity. His writing invites you into the miraculous mundane inviting everyone to play with the notion that maybe, just maybe, there is a bit of mystic in each of us waiting to be discovered. I am grateful for Kevin's book, *The Making of a Mystic,* as it gives us a companion on the journey of rediscovering our own inner mystic."

Sarah Heath
Author of *What's your Story? Seeing your life through God's eyes* and *The Authenticity Challenge.* Host of the "Making Spaces" podcast and co-host of "REVcovery" and "Your favorite Aunts" podcasts.

THE MAKING

OF A

MYSTIC

MY JOURNEY WITH MUSHROOMS

MY LIFE AS A PASTOR

AND WHY IT'S OKAY FOR EVERYONE TO RELAX

KEVIN SWEENEY

Copyright © 2022 by Kevin Sweeney

First Edition

Cover design and layout by Rafael Polendo (polendo.net)
Cover illustration by robin.ph (shutterstock.com)
Author photo by Wes Hodge

Unless otherwise identified, all Scripture quotations in this publication are taken from the Holy Bible, New International Version®, NIV®. Copyright ©1973, 1978, 1984, 2011 by Biblica, Inc.™ Used by permission of Zondervan. All rights reserved worldwide. www.zondervan.com The "NIV" and "New International Version" are trademarks registered in the United States Patent and Trademark Office by Biblica, Inc.™

ISBN 978-1-957007-14-4

This volume is printed on acid free paper and meets ANSI Z39.48 standards.

Printed in the United States of America

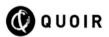 QUOIR

Published by Quoir
Oak Glen, California

www.quoir.com

DEDICATION

To my love, **Christine**.
Thank you for seeing me before I knew what it meant to be seen.

ACKNOWLEDGEMENTS

Mikayla and True for making me a daddy and calling me further into love.

My parents for supporting me on my journey, even when it made no sense.

Livvy for always picking up the phone.

Doc Watkins for introducing me to the beauty and power of the Black prophetic tradition.

Phil and Jen for being with us from the beginning.

Steve Carter for taking the time that summer.

Costa Mesa Fam (you know who you are) for loving us into the future.

Imagine Church for making me into something I always knew I could be.

Larry and Hoku for your courage, commitment, and friendship.

Rafael and Quoir for responding to my email so quickly.

The land and people of Hawai'i for welcoming and embracing me.

TABLE OF CONTENTS

INTRODUCTION

A few nights after New Year's Eve in 2003, I thought that I might die.

Or at least, need to be checked into a psychiatric unit, put in a straight jacket, and be under professional medical watch for a while.

I knew things were about to get bad.

At about midnight on that defining night, I had eaten more mushrooms than I had ever eaten, I was with my best friend Squirrel (I should have known it would go bad), and within an hour I was tiptoeing on the edge of darkness, sanity, and what felt like death.

Actually, let's hold off on that story and begin a different way. I promise I'll come back to it.

What does it mean to be a mystic?

The mystic is the one who
trusts God,
trusts life,
trusts death,
trusts light,
trusts darkness,

trusts good,
trusts bad,
trusts joy,
trusts pain,
and ultimately just trusts.

When you experience so much resurrection on the other side of death, indestructible union with Spirit as you befriend your pain, increasing inner spaciousness after each form of acceptance, further joy after all the forgiveness, and the radical liberation in love through letting go, you do not have to try harder to trust.

You just do.

There's simply nothing left to fear, mistrust, or avoid.

The mystic feels safe in this universe because they know that to take your first breath is to be carried over the threshold into your new home. The mystic has awakened to the astonishing realization that we live in an atmosphere where there is no judgment, no shame, no contempt, no need to prove your worth, no need to fight for your place, and nothing you have to do to earn the right to just be.

But before we get ahead of ourselves.

For people who think claiming to be a mystic is self-congratulatory, or self-aggrandizing in any way, trust me, it's not. You get no credit for the silent pioneering of consciousness, no applause for the boundary breaking exploration of the interior universe, and no pity for the time you spend in that holy inner sanctuary weeping over the world, on behalf of the world.

Nobody knows, nobody cares, it doesn't give you any clout on a social or cultural level, and it definitely does nothing to increase your finances.

Trust me.

This beautifully maddening journey is like carrying around one of the great secrets of the universe inside your heart, knowing 99.9% of people are not interested in it.

The irony built into the journey is too hilarious, and I love it and cherish it deeply.

When the great mystic Rumi speaks of his relationship with the divine, he says, "You dance inside my chest where no one sees you."

This interior dance dissolves the lines between sacred and secular, unveils the connection between the cosmic and the personal, collapses the barriers between heaven and earth, and exposes love and light as the substance of our very existence.

Yes. Life with God is a dance between the infinite and the intimate.

Another reason why the path of the mystic is one that will never be celebrated is that this mysterious path is one that is defined by death. The mystics are who they are because they have wept. They have wrestled with God, they have fought with reality and they have suffered deeply. They have also have held those unnerving spaces of darkness long enough, and have witnessed their illusions die frequently enough, to allow love to completely undo them and save them.

To be a mystic is to attend your own funeral over and over, but also to discover that the funeral is actually the entrance to the party.

Or, as Richard Rohr says, you learn to see "Death as the price for resurrection."

The mystic no longer has to wrestle with God and fight reality like they once did, but that's only because they have accepted the presence of pain, let go of every expectation, and tearfully and cheerfully surrendered their life along the way.

The peace the mystic has in public is born out of the tears they have shed in private.

+ + +

A bit about me.

From the beginning, my faith was an unconditional and universal "Yes" spoken into the center of my being directly from God. There were no youth group pastors walking alongside of me, no sermons to help make sense of my life, and no altar call that provided a defining moment with Jesus.

Instead, it was my own journey within, wisdom being spoken through creation itself, and a psychedelic experience gone wrong that conspired together to clear out the way for the infinite love of God beyond to become the intimate life of God born within.

The revolutionary Catholic mystic Thomas Merton said, "If we seek paradise outside ourselves, we cannot have praise in our hearts."

This simple, but radical truth from Merton was the engine that drove me to give up everything to pursue truth when I was seventeen. More than anything else, I dreamt of freedom and longed for peace, but I knew that the only way for these temporary experiences to become a permanent path was if they were not contingent upon anything outside of me.

Freedom had to be an inside job, peace had to be a part of me, and joy could not be connected to anything that could be taken from me.

Truth.
Authenticity.
Liberation.

And the desire to walk on the solid ground of what is real was all that mattered to me.

+ + +

Good Will Hunting has always been one of my favorite movies.

There are myriad reasons why I love this movie, connect with the character, and find so much of myself in the story. The character uses cynicism and a superabundance of knowledge to avoid emotional risk, failure, and the unavoidable complexity and messiness of real life.

I have been there at times.

It puts on display an archetypal journey for the people who tend to live the majority of their lives in their minds to courageously translate all of the knowledge they have acquired into concrete love, work, and contribution for the world.

This is my journey too.

But the one scene that stands out to me that captures so much of what I have felt since I was eighteen, was the one where Matt Damon's character Will, explains to his girlfriend what it feels like to learn so easily.

After answering a question from her about organic chemistry, she wonders and asks about his ability to understand so much intellectually. Here is the heart of his response.

Will says,

"When Beethoven looked at a piano, it just made sense to him…. Beethoven, Mozart, when they saw it, they could just play."

And after saying he has no capacity to play the piano at all, his girlfriend interjects and says, "But you can do my Organic Chemistry paper in under an hour."

And Will finishes his explanation by saying,

"Well, when it came to stuff like that, I could always just play."

I have always deeply resonated with this part of the scene, and this sentiment about being able to just play. For a long time, I didn't know why. I wasn't a genius like he was, I didn't have a photographic memory, and I damn sure would never casually read and learn about topics like Organic Chemistry (I didn't even pass biology in High School).

For years, I did not know exactly why I felt such deep solidarity reverberating through my being when I heard that.

Then eventually, I understood.

That is how I felt when it came to the inner life and the unfolding of consciousness.

Since I was about seventeen, I knew I could "just play," and that some of the most complex psychological, spiritual, and emotional dynamics just made sense to me. And not only could I see simplicity at the heart of so much interior complexity, but I could untangle, overcome, and transcend internal barriers with a casual ease.

My growth was still painful—like it is for all of us—but always felt simple.

To be clear, there is so much of life I am absolutely horrible at.

It might take me weeks to respond to one email (sorry!), I am a mess with organizational leadership (six years into leading a church, I would sometimes still google "what to do in a meeting"), and it wasn't until my mid twenties that I learned an oil change was different from just putting more oil in your car (although technically, that is changing your oil).

But when it came to developing awareness of and differentiating from my false self, that felt simple.

When it came to entering into the dark night of the soul and dying to my ego, that seemed natural.

When it came to the movement from an initial encounter with God to a life steadily lived in Christ, that felt normal.

And the dismantling of defense mechanisms, the vision to see that dysfunctional symptoms are always born out of a part of your shadow, and the overcoming of these shadow elements through the bringing of them into the light of God just clicked for me internally.

When it came to this stuff, I could always just play.

+ + +

From eighteen (when I first encountered God) until twenty-eight (when we started a church), I did not do very much. I got married, got some degrees, traveled, and read virtually non-stop, but what I mean is that I did not contribute or create much in a quantifiable sense. This is why I say I spent a decade in silence in solitude.

Every day in silence, and each moment in my invisibility, I got to ask from the depths of my being, is this universal "Yes" from God being spoken over my life truly enough?

And in every silent space I sat in, my own response of "yes" would get stronger and take root deeper.

Ken Wilber said, "The great mystical religions always mention practices that quiet the small self we pretend we are—which causes all our pain and suffering—and awaken the Great Self that is our own true ground, goal, and destiny."

When most people my age were grinding, grasping, and working hard to get ahead, I was quieting, awakening and letting go of the need to be ahead.

While old friends were playing college sports on national television, I would learn how to breathe deeply, and know the Spirit of God was with me.

While my peers were getting jobs at churches, preaching their first sermons, or getting into Ph.D programs, I was sitting on the side of a cliff where no one could see me, learning what it means to be truly seen.

While others were making a name for themselves, I was quietly receiving a new name from God.

So for ten years, I resisted the temptation to lapse back into my false self and try to re-create a special name for myself, and instead spent an entire decade of my life receiving the Word of silence, becoming the unified field, and trusting the name God had given me.

During the season of life where other people were getting ahead, passing me by, starting churches, starting Ph.D programs, getting book deals, and making connections, I would watch all of it happening while staying still.

Why would it matter if people are passing me by if they're not going where I'm going?

+ + +

This book is not an autobiography, but it is, in part, autobiographical. It is not intended to tell the story of my life, but it does tell stories from my life, in order to speak some universal truth through my life.

Some of the stories of others in here are literal, others have details that have been changed to protect people's identity. All of them, I hope, enable the reader to not only see a future filled with more joy, but to also recognize everything that is getting in the way.

Most people talk about what we see, this is more about how we see.

Most people talk about the objects that arise in our awareness, this is more about the nature of the awareness itself.

Most people talk about the why and the what of spirituality, this book is more about the how.

These words flow out of the interconnected streams of ancient wisdom, modern knowledge, personal and cultural location, the perennial mystical tradition, the biblical narrative, and deep personal experience that comes together in the Spirit.

Each chapter is like an integral part of the unified wisdom that I have suffered for in ways you can only understand if you've felt it yourself, glimpses of the freedom that I have shed tears for when no one was watching, and pieces of heaven I left with after fighting my way through hell.

I know.

Sounds dramatic.

No need to worry. I don't take myself that seriously.

And although the personal stories shared can be placed in order on the timeline of my life, they are not in order in this book. Since my intention is not to tell my life story, the critical moments of my life are scattered through out the pages without any attempt to line them up chronologically. But even without the order of events, I am confident you will still be able to get a feel for the journey that made me.

My hope is that the personal stories of my life can become an open door to step in and see the cosmic story that is unfolding through all of life.

So, some chapters you may connect with in a deeply personal way and other chapters might be of no interest to you at all.

That's okay.

+ + +

When I was about twenty-four years old, I went on a walk one night.

It was a contemplative walk—not going anywhere in particular, breathing and simply being present, and having a rhythmic conversation with God.

As I was was walking and smoking a Black & Mild cigar (for nostalgic reasons) I had this profound and unforgettable exchange. The back and forth went like this.

I said out loud, "It's one of those moments where you just know."

Then another voice said, "Know what?"

To which I responded "I don't know, but you just do."

So, as you read this book and go on this journey my hope is that you will just know. And if you wonder and ask, know what?

My response is, "I don't know, but I hope you do."

PELOTON, CHEERLEADING FOR THE EGO, AND TRANSFORMATION

I recently overheard a phone conversation between my wife Christine and one of her best friends Kristin. I couldn't hear everything they were saying, but from what I did hear, the conversation included how Peloton instructors are like pastors, marathon running, hustling, and conquering and overcoming pain.

Here's something you need to know; my wife and Kristin have a similar flavor of personality and many shared traits—ambitious, hard working, determined, loving, and they both possess a seemingly endless inner supply of energy reserves.

If life was a game, then in every conversation they have, I think they beat it.

So as the original conversation was ending, the conversation approached an unexpected turn. After all of the talk about overcoming and conquering pain, Kristin asked my wife a question: "With all of this, how does it translate into conquering anxiety?" To which my wife replied, "That one I haven't completely figured out yet."

Now, my wife Christine is a Marriage and Family Therapist, a pastor, highly self aware, and a natural healer for people. Kristin has done social work, worked with people in suicide prevention, and understands much of the inner life. So, the ending of that conversation is in no way a slight to them, rather it is an expression of the different inner mechanics required for overcoming things with the strength of the ego, and overcoming the ego itself.

Soon after this conversation, my wife talked me into doing one guided twenty minute interval run with one of her and Kristin's favorite Peloton instructors. In my defense, I live in Hawaii and it was disgustingly humid outside at the time. So by the time my run ended, I was lying down on the front lawn of an apartment tower that wasn't my own. I wanted to give up multiple times, when I lied down in the grass at the end I could feel my heart beating in my face, and I had a head ache the rest of the day.

Did I mention I have a really low tolerance for physical pain?

What struck me the most about that Peloton run was the way the instructor spoke during the workout. She was energetic, encouraging, inspirational, wove in spiritual language seamlessly, and used every cliché imaginable.

"Don't think, just do."

"You're a part of my wolf pack."

"Wear your crown."

"The hustle in me recognizes the hustle in you."

There were a lot more that are too much for me to even type.

Let's just say the very comments that get my wife and Kristin all pumped up make me want to throw my phone at the wall.

This kind of communicating is powerful, inspirational, and people love it. I actually believe the same reasons why people love this kind of motivational workout talk is why people love the most famous Christian preachers as well.

As I was running, I kept thinking that if you sprinkle in a few Bible verses, this has the same feel of a lot of popular sermons.

This is about tapping into grit, accessing our tenacity, focusing our mind, maintaining a positive view of ourselves, and being able to push through barriers with our own strength and our own will. This is the energy within the idea that we must refuse to lose.

This is what makes great athletes.

This is what fuels powerful CEOs.

This is what allows pastors to build empires.

Going back to the question about overcoming anxiety Kristin asked my wife, and looking at this kind of inspirational communication, we see that while this communication is valuable for certain dimensions of our life—namely anything that requires will power or ego strength—it is also extremely limited as well.

Why? Well…

You can't grit your way out of heartbreak.

You can't try your way out of trauma.

You can't will your way past anxiety.

A refuse to lose mindset does not help when what is required for growth and movement are the acceptance of hurt and loss. If the only way to evolve through certain stages of our life is through our ability to embrace loss, then the refuse to lose mindset is the very thing that will keep you stuck.

When it comes to the ambitions of the ego, the need for will power, inspiration and motivation will help you work harder. But in the further journey of radical transformation and healing, motivation cannot guide you, and inspiration alone is unable to lead you.

A driven young woman telling me "my hustle recognizes your hustle" won't help me when I need to grieve my greatest emotional wounds, or let go of my most cherished expectations on life.

So often, what we seek in inspiration is only going to be found through transformation.

+ + +

Our church Imagine, has always had different waves of athletes from the University of Hawaii come through and become a part of the church. A few years back, there were two quarterbacks from the football team who were part of Imagine at the same time, both of whom I was pretty close to.

One was on scholarship and a redshirt, who sat out his first year of eligibility, and was now the backup quarterback as a freshman. He had high expectations to become the starter, had the body type of a true NFL quarterback, and was young, hungry, and waiting for his chance to prove himself.

The other was a walk on who took four years off after High School before going to college, someone who had tried out for the team multiple times, never suited up for a game, and was now getting ready for his final year where he was finally going to have a spot on the roster. He had work ethic of Rudy, and with the compassion and wisdom he carried, and was happy to have a positive role in the lives of players on the team, even though it was possible he would never get in the game.

I remember how different the individual conversations I would have with each of them were that year.

As the younger one was waiting to get his chance to start, he would share his frustration, his eagerness to establish himself, and his insatiable desire to make a name for himself. Near the end of one particular conversation we were having on campus, I told him he needs to work harder than everyone else, be more hungry than anyone else, and not let anybody in college football train harder than him. I would remind him who he was, how capable he was, that I was with him no matter what, and that his time was coming.

The conversation was inspiration, encouragement, motivation, and support.

The nature of the conversations between the older quarterback and I were nothing like the conversations I was having with the younger one. He would ask questions about why a part of him needed to be on the team so bad, we would explore what it was that drove him so incessantly to succeed in sports, he would ask daring questions like: Who am I without sports? What does it mean to be grounded in an identity that is truly and only in Christ? Why do I need this?

The first conversation was encouraging, inspiring, and empowering the ego.

The second one was about questioning, recognizing, and overcoming the ego.

The first conversation was about maintaining a positive view the self on the way to success.

The second one was about dying to the self on the way to freedom.

Hustle and hard work can establish a positive social image for you, but they cannot help you touch the freedom that transcends any other person's perspective of you. Determination and will can put you in a position of power, but they cannot help you experience the real power of not needing power at all. Tenacity, relentlessness, and drive can build empires, fulfill dreams, and make you powerful and famous, but they do not have the power to lead you to the radical liberation that only exists on the other side of the funeral for the false self.

Or, to put it another way.

Michael Jordan can show us the absolute commitment needed to win, but he can not show us the radical liberation that comes from relinquishing the ego need to win itself.

+ + +

Ken Wilber makes a distinction between translative spirituality and transformative spirituality.

Translative spirituality is usually where the journey begins. Here, the self is given an improved way of viewing reality, a healthier way of relating to God, a new way of seeing themselves, and a more compassionate way of looking at humanity.

So when the pastor or teacher says, "God loves you, and God demonstrates this love in Jesus. You are worthy of good, capable of great of things, and every human being is your neighbor," that can be a powerful, even revolutionary experience. To believe we are loved by God, to start to trust that we are worthy and capable, and to be called to see every human being as a neighbor to care for, this can be a brand new way of translating and seeing the world.

The belief in a loving God can give us a positive sense of self, can ground our experience in a chaotic and uncertain world, can empower us to act, and can expand our view of inclusion and compassion.

The main task of translative spirituality is to provide a set of beliefs that creates a new lens to see God, your self, humanity, and our world in a positive way.

This is where almost everyone begins.

And thats a good thing.

Even though the translative role religion plays in our life is essential and empowering, the transformative mode of spirituality is how we take a monumental leap into a depth of freedom that was previously unimaginable.

Which is why Wilber says that it is "not a matter of belief, but the death of the believer."

And why I say transformative spirituality is not about beliefs for the self, it is about the death of the self (Which, I am aware is essentially the same thing).

This evolutionary movement is to go from finding comfort and a sense of stability for your self, to awakening to the infinite grace on the other side of the death of the self. This massive transition enlightens the eyes of the heart to see that it is not new ideas that will liberate you, it is only the transcending of what you perviously thought was you, that will allow you to release into the infinite presence of God.

The first step will make you feel safe (for a while), the second one leaves you undone.

The first step puts you together, the second one takes you a part.

The first step is creating a name for yourself, the second one is realizing that this name means nothing when you are face to face with God.

This is why translative spirituality does a great job helping you begin, creating excitement and momentum for the journey, but ultimately can not take you all the way on the Christ journey.

If leading is more translating, inspiring, and empowering the self, without ever transforming, overcoming, and dying to the self, then we are only leading people into the first half of life.

Through the past fifteen years, most sermons I have heard are encouragement for the ego, management techniques for the false self, and a path of holding together the very self Jesus said needs to die.

Most preaching is cheerleading for the ego.

Which is why Joel Osteen is not bad.

He's like the sweet uncle who sees you, gives you a big hug, and says, "You're doing a great job little buddy. Keep going." But what the further journey requires of us is to let go of the very self that Osteen is smiling at and encouraging.

You cannot overcome the ego with the determination of the ego. No, you overcome the ego by dis-identifying with it, surrendering it, and moving beyond it altogether. Which is why Wilber writes, "But with radical transformation, the self itself is inquired into, looked into, grabbed by its throat and literally throttled to death."

In other words, the ego does not need encouragement, it needs a eulogy.

Paul Smith accurately claims that, "We will choose comforting the self rather than dying to the self every time. That is, unless we have a tradition which pushes us to ego death."

The inspiring, energetic, well crafted sermons that function as cheerleading for the ego can fill stadiums, but they do not carry the potential to lead human beings beyond to the second half of their life.

+ + +

There was another young man from the football team I became close to a few years ago. He had just finished his football career in college, and was walking closer to that terrifying edge where the thing that you felt made you distinctively you for a long time might be coming to a close. Although he still had some chances to try and extend his football career professionally, he was also realistic about the possibility of this being the end.

Through facing the void left by the death of the old self, the overwhelming feelings that arise in its absence, and the entrusting of this uncertain moment into the inexhaustible compassion of God, this young man would be born again beyond that old ego identity. He would go on to do Teach for America, finish his master's degree, and move home to the Big Island and re-invest in the lives of the kids who are growing up in the same tough environment he did.

He saw for himself that after one monumental step of transcending his old self, there was more life on the other side.

When he finished grad school, I sent him a pair of Jordan 1's as a gift, and in that gift was a short note.

"Let's allow our favorite athletes to inspire us to be great, and let's allow Jesus to show us what greatness truly is."

In other words, let's allow our favorite athletes and cultural figures to motivate us through the determination of the self, but have the eyes to see that the greatest depth, joy, and sacredness of life is born out of the death of that very self.

When we eventually are confronted with the wall that exists at the edge of our own willpower, respond to the beckoning of the Spirit that draws us beyond our ego, and we are ready to listen to Jesus' call to die to our self, we will be born again as the Great Self that is before, beneath, and beyond everything we thought we were.

Here, and only here in this open field of union and you will know:

It's not hustling, it's healing.

It's not willing it, its waking up.

It's not trying harder, its being loved better.

So let's appreciate the Peloton energy and clichés for keeping our self going, let's acknowledge the cheerleading for the ego that so many pastors and leaders have done for us, and let's allow the most driven athletes and successful cultural figures to inspire our selves to be great.

Let's just always remember that the boundless freedom of Spirit is always on the other side of the death of the self most people are trying to inspire.

MUSHROOMS AND MISSIONARIES

Thomas Merton was one of the greatest mystics of the Twentieth Century.

At a critical crossroads in his journey, he met the Hindu monk Mahanambrata Brahmachari, who told him to read The Confessions of St. Augustine and Thomas à Kempis' Imitation of Christ.

A Hindu Monk tells a young white male from the West, who would eventually become one of the greatest Christian mystics ever, to read Christian writers in order to guide him further on his spiritual journey.

Very strange.

And I love it.

The guidance of this Hindu monk, pointing him toward some of the classic spiritual texts of the Christian tradition became a moment for the young Merton on his journey toward becoming a monk, toward the truth, and ultimately toward Christ.

This brilliant Hindu Monk was an unexpected missionary for Jesus.

I'm pretty sure that was not in his job description.

If we simplify the term missionary (while acknowledging the obvious and urgent need to disentangle the white supremist, imperialist and oppressive knot that word is stuck in), then a missionary is one who points others further toward Christ.

The missionary is not the point, the missionary embraces the humble role of pointing—pointing people to Christ, to the source, to the creator, to love, and to salvation. Which is why it is accurate to say that for Merton, Mahanambrata Brahmachari was a missionary showing him the way forward, which ultimately led him to Christ.

With that said, mushrooms were a missionary for me.

Which always creates weird conversations when people ask me what it was that lead me to Christ.

I started eating psychedelic mushrooms when I was sixteen years old, and within the next couple years I would end up eating mushrooms on ten different occasions. These experiences were some of the most powerful happenings in my spiritual journey, and some of the most vital events for my life.

And while these experiences were critical elements of my spiritual quest, I would also simply trip out and have a lot of the classic experiences people have on psychedelics.

I would have the sense of enchantment and euphoria, and the mind bending visuals that come from hallucinating on psylocibin.

I would see walls turning inside out over and over until it felt like I was seeing into an entirely different dimension.

I would hug my girlfriend at the time (Who is now my wife! How she stayed with me through those times is beyond me) and not only feel the electricity of connection, but actually see the power of connection as we were together—it's bright blue if you were wondering.

I would watch a movie in my room alone and see the TV shelf bend with me in my chair as if it was mirroring my exact movement.

I would watch the movie "Alice in Wonderland" with my friends (which was allegedly written by somebody on a psychedelic trip) and at the end of it, think to myself, "I get it." (That always makes me laugh.)

I would sit outside of a party at a friend's house calmly in a chair, and simultaneously listen to four or five different conversations happening around me, and mysteriously be able to comprehend every single one.

I would stand on a porch with friends smoking cigarettes in mind blowing awe at the miracle of verbal communication.

I would have moments where I was outside myself watching myself interact with other people, and have this destabilizing experience of hearing my voice from their perspective (I still get subtle and jarring flashbacks of this experience to this day).

I would wake up from blacking out on top of a mountain and regain my consciousness before my sight, and think I went blind (that one wasn't as much fun!).

Like everyone else, I had these euphoric and entertaining experiences while on mushrooms, but it was more than that.

At sixteen, while on mushrooms, I first developed a radical third person perspective of self awareness during an out of body experience that would help define my faith.

On mushrooms, I began to inhabit the universe as the enchanted, spirit soaked, mystery shaped reality that it is.

On mushrooms, I discovered that is was possible for the mind to truly be at peace.

On mushrooms, my growing dissatisfaction with the cycle of gratifying the ego was increased, my intuition that something deeper was happening in life than just the pursuit of money, sex, and fame was enhanced, while a steady flow of wisdom was starting to present herself to me in powerful ways.

On mushrooms, I was gaining access to just how vast, beautiful, and essential our interior universe is—and this access would never allow me to return to my normal life in the same way.

I had these profound awakening experiences, life changing visions, and gained so much wisdom while on mushrooms, but it was even more than that.

I always sensed something within the mushroom experiences saying to me, "yes, but keep going."

During this exciting and pioneering new season of my life, all of these profound psychedelic experiences were not taking place in a vacuum. During this two year period of my life, while most of my friends were just partying and trying to make it through High School, I was moving toward, already in, and eventually trying to find a way out of a deep and dark existential crisis.

Let's just say my Senior year of High School was really weird.

I was realizing everything I ever wanted through sports, music, and popularity was just the pursuit of an insecure ego that wanted to be seen as special or receive approval. I was beginning to accept that my inability to be sober was a problem, and that I did, in fact, use drugs and alcohol as a way of coping with reality. I was starting to disconnect from relationships because I was tired of using, manipulating, and objectifying others. I just felt done spending time with people who had no clue who I actually was.

I was done with everything that felt fake, and only wanted to know what was real. I was in the center of that infamous chapter of so many people's lives where you have everything and it feels like nothing.

Thomas Merton said, "…the prophetic life is that a person rocks the boat, not by telling slaves to be free, but by telling people who think they're free that they're slaves."

Or was that Morpheus in *The Matrix*?

Either way, at eighteen, I knew I wasn't free.

I also know I would give everything up, and let go of anything I needed in order to know what real freedom was. Here, I began a conscious quest for truth.

So here I was, on this spiritual journey for truth, and living with this deep conviction that I am either going to discover that there is something real here, some larger cosmic story I can give my life to, or accept the painful truth that this is all arbitrary, and that there is, in fact, no meaningful narrative arch in the universe. I was going though this chapter knowing that if the latter was was true, I thought I might kill myself.

Who wants to suffer if there's no meaning?

Now, back to the mushrooms.

These mushroom experiences were one of the main places I looked to for a sense of grounding, and a vision for the goal of my future.

They were the missionary showing me the way.

They were a signpost pointing me to the future I couldn't see, the freedom I desired but wasn't sure existed, and to the truth I hoped for, but knew wasn't guaranteed. They would give me a glimpse, while I knew the goal was much further ahead. They would allow me to see just enough to give me the energy and the excitement to keep moving forward. They would bless me with just enough of a taste of the possibilities of freedom to keep going ahead toward what felt like the promises of an entirely different future.

The mushrooms kept saying "yes, but keep going."

Trust what you see, do not settle for anything less than fullness and freedom, have the courage to continue.

I could sense in the depth of my being that the mushrooms were confirming my journey, letting me know I was on the right path, and giving me the hope to keep going. The mushrooms were the missionary humbly whispering to me, "You are on the edge of discovering the secret of the universe."

Or, quite possibly,

between the weed, psychedelics, other drugs, heavy drinking, isolation, and silent existential crisis, I had to accept the scary possibility that I was starting to become unhinged.

(I have to laugh at that.)

So while I embraced this possibility (especially when I was parked at night time on the side of the road smoking blunts and talking to myself), at a deeper level, I knew exactly what I was doing.

But as the crescendo for this season of exploration approached, and with mushrooms as my guide, a few days after New Year's Eve, at eighteen years old, I would have this spontaneous awakening moment with God that would transform my consciousness and life forever.

I went from crying out in the darkness to seeing the light.
From exploration to experience.
From wanting to see the truth to being seen by the truth.

The signs that kept pointing me forward faded into the rearview mirror on my path as I came face to face with the Source itself.

(You can read about that experience in the chapter titled "More Mushrooms and the Most Important of My Life").

+ + +

After my first conscious experience of God, I never did psychedelics or hard drugs again (it took me a couple years to quit smoking weed).

The mushrooms were missionaries pointing me beyond themselves to the ultimate source, and on that unforgettable night, I had encountered the source itself. The mushrooms were giving me glimpses of the goal, and in that first awakening moment, I knew I had experienced that ultimate reality. The mushrooms were a signpost showing me the way to the destination, and when I had that first experience of light and love, I knew the destination was my true home.

They led me to love.
They led me to truth.
They led me to light.

They led me to the only thing I ever experienced that was real—God.

And because of the infinite mystery of God, what was powerful about this experience of the source, was that the end of my quest actually felt like another beginning.

Alan Watts has one of the most well known quotes about psychedelics and awakening:

> "[P]sychedelic experience is only a glimpse of genuine mystical insight, but a glimpse which can be matured and deepened by the various ways of meditation in which drugs are no longer

necessary or useful. When you get the message, hang up the phone. For psychedelic drugs are simply instruments, like microscopes, telescopes, and telephones. The biologist does not sit with eye permanently glued to the microscope; he goes away and works on what he has seen."

When you get the message, hang up the phone.

This is exactly what I did. I never went back to the sign to look for directions. I never went looking for the missionary to point the way. I never went back to the phone to check for more messages once I heard the truth.

I never ate mushrooms again.

Even when six months later, when I thought about doing mushrooms again because I was aware of how good they can feel, I had this deep conviction that to do mushrooms after the experience of Spirit was actually to betray Spirit.

Wouldn't that be me saying that the source isn't enough, that grace isn't enough, that God isn't enough?

I refused to ever do that.

To go back to that which was pointing me beyond itself would not only be me betraying the

Spirit, it would be me betraying my own integrity.

When you get the message, hang up the phone.

That's exactly what I did. With a smile that was virtually unnoticeable to those around me, and a transformed sense of Self that knew it had been born again, I hung up the phone for good and began the real journey of living this message.

+ + +

The real work of transformation, and the further journey toward freedom, does not happen during the psychedelic trip, it always happens after.

On Monday, when the magic fades.

On Tuesday, when you start to forget the deep insight you received.

On Wednesday, when you lose the inner stillness you felt.

On Thursday, when you're thinking about when you're going to trip again.

And especially on Friday, when you feel like you again.

This is where you see whether the spiritual high is going to ever become solid ground.

The great world religion scholar Huston Smith, and one of the four men featured in the amazing book *The Harvard Psychedelic Club*, which traces the origins and history of the contemporary psychedelic movement, wrote in his beautiful memoir, *Tales of Wonder*,

"Entheogens [another name for psychedelics] might be able to produce a religious experience, but not a religious life."

The real work that extends beyond the religious experience comes from consistent practices that enable you to return to and remain in the Spirit. The real work is whether or not you're going to face your own shadow and feel those painful things that arise all the way though to the other side. The real work is confronting, naming, and letting go of all of the illusions that you have believed. The real work is surrendering all expectations on life, and I truly mean all. The real work is having the courage to heal the deep wounds that you carry within you. The real work is always some form of letting go.

These things that most of the time don't feel very spiritual at all—these are always the defining markers of the real journey. So when I see people using spiritual language and still returning to psychedelics hundreds of times, sometimes

I see people who want a short cut to a religious experience instead of following the long road of a religious life.

I see people who keep picking up the phone even though they already got the message.

I see people who want to keep having another one night stand with Spirit instead of making the faithful commitment to life with God.

And I'm not judging them for that desire, but I am making the distinction between that desire for a guaranteed experience through psychedelics, and the path I'm focusing on that always knows these things are at best, signposts pointing the way ahead.

So, based on my experience with mushrooms and even in my day to day role as a pastor today, can I say psychedelics are completely evil?

Of course not.

Do I actually recommend them to people?

No.

Do I understand why people get into them?

Absolutely.

Do I believe they lead most people to truly de-center their ego and embrace an enlightened, transformed, and loving path?

No.

Do I see research that reveals positive therapeutic effects?

Yes.

The majority of people who I ate mushrooms and tripped out with are not enlightened gurus, they are not leading the culture as voices for justice, they are not leading activists in compassion, and they are not people who I see as being liberated from the overwhelming power of their ego.

And yet, I also know there are smart, sincere, and caring people who are continuing the research and exploration of psychedelics and plant medicine on behalf of humanity.

In the end, for most people the psychedelic trip may just become a momentary door to a great party, but for me, they were a wise missionary pointing me beyond themselves to the ultimate celebration in God.

They were the signs pointing me to the ocean, which enabled me to get in the water, and eventually wake up to life in the water, and eventually into life as the water.

With so much left to be said, maybe I should write more about this in the future.

Actually, never mind.

BADGES OF SHAME

Costco has one of the best return policies on the planet.

They will take back anything.

I know this because the Costco card my wife and I use is an old account in my name. Which means all of the times my wife wanted to return something, I ended up being the one who would have to stand in line, get to the front and look that worker dead in their eyes and let them know I was there to return some brussel sprouts.

Of course my wife would tell me something was wrong with them when we got them, but we all know the truth.

We just never used them and they went bad.

While I was returning them, no matter what they thought about me while I was doing it, I knew they were going to give me a refund; and I also knew there was a chance we would buy more vegetables we wouldn't end up using with that refunded money from the previous vegetables we didn't use.

It's a dangerous cycle.

I remember at one point in the first year and a half of starting Imagine, my wife and I were coming to the end of the month and our financial situation was looking a bit problematic. And by problematic, I mean we didn't have any money to buy food for the rest of the month.

The first year of starting Imagine, every month was a struggle.

Even though we didn't have any money at the time, we did have a couple wavestorms laying on the side of our house. If you're not familiar, a wavestorm is an impossibly thick, eight foot, soft top surfboard you can buy from Costco for a hundred dollars.

If you surf a lot, a wave storm is not your main board, it's just something you keep around for friends to use when they visit, to play around on when the surf is small, or to take out on days when it's huge and you want to get weird. But, due to our financial condition, and Costco's return policy, what we saw in these boards was just over two hundred dollars we could use for groceries until the end of the month. So Christine and I decided to return the boards, get the money, and celebrate that we made it through another month financially in this adventure of starting a church.

This is one of those moments that we want to naturally wear as a badge of shame.

Badges of shame are the struggles we hide, the moments we keep to ourselves, the things we have to do that we think make us less credible, those parts of us that we get embarrassed by because we believe they put on display that we are not as far as we should be. A badge of shame is something we silently wear, hoping that no one else notices because we believe it takes away from what we are doing, and even more deeply, from who we are.

It's the side hustle nobody would ever imagine you still have to do to make your life work while you're making your dream happen.

It's the slow struggle of trying to make the business happen behind the scenes of your creative life, knowing how embarrassed you would be if others knew just how messy things really were for you organizationally.

It's showing up alone to the bar on another Sunday morning to open for church while it's dark out, and having to begin to clear the floor by yourself because the couple people who are supposed to help are late (that one might just be me!).

Or, it's having to decide between your wavestorms or groceries after you've taken an impossible risk with your life to start a church you believe in.

While I understand the ego's default response of immediately wearing all of these decisions as badges of shame, the truth is that they should be worn as the exact opposite.

What we treat as badges of shame, should be worn as badges of courage.

All of these embarrassing realities are actually the necessary things most people are unwilling to do, and the sacrifices people are unwilling to make in order to live authentically.

It's not humiliating, it's simply embracing the hard parts of the adventurous life that define whether or not we are going to keep growing and creating. These are not decisions we make that we're supposed to anxiously wear like badges of shame, hoping that no one ever finds out—no! These are badges of courage that should be worn with honor because each one is another statement we make to the world about how we are not going to settle.

Telemon of Arcadia said, "It's one thing to study war, and another to live the warrior's life."

In our culture and in our vocational struggle, the warrior is the one who will never settle. She is the one who knows she is here to make something, to create something, to contribute something to the unfolding flow of this universe. She is the one who will do whatever it takes to ensure that her offering does not remain within.

What feels like a badge of shame is symbol of your commitment.

What feels like a badge of shame is a statement about your unwillingness to settle.

What feels like a badge of shame is the very decision that defines whether or not your true voice is going to be heard.

I look back at all of those moments in the bar alone turning the lights on and moving the chairs and tables while I set up by myself, or having to trade in our wavestorms for groceries when we were almost thirty. I remember how in those moments I could feel a part of my ego contract because I would want to feel embarrassed. Like I should be further along as a leader, like my friends who were pastors might feel disappointed in me because I wasn't more organized than I was, and that this somehow proved to others that I wasn't as capable as they assumed.

But thankfully, I also remember how in those moments—while acknowledging I could have always done things better—I was deeply grateful and honored to have a vision wide enough to fight for, and to be able to have something I cared about enough to transform all of my badges of shame into badges of courage.

So know that whatever embarrassing or humiliating thing you have to do right now that feels like a badge of shame isn't actually the problem, the problem is that your badge simply has the wrong label on it.

PEOPLE AND PATTERNS

Without forgiveness, people get stuck.

Without learning the art of acceptance, people end up resisting reality and struggling to force the unwelcome material of life into a container that doesn't exist. Without being aware of what needs to be let go of, we end up falling into the trap of holding onto the very things that are getting in the way of the freedom we desire.

Here is something interesting.

The paths of letting go and acceptance are not defined by a duration of time that passes, they are defined by an intentional process we go through.

While forgiveness and letting go both have a mysterious energy, there is still a structure or mechanics to the experience. And like everything else, the more you understand it and do it, the easier it becomes. The easier it becomes, the faster you're able to do it next time.

Whether you choose to let go or accept something in five minutes or in five years, the process required for freedom and growth remain the same. If you wait five years, the same step that is eventually taken was the very step that needed to be taken five days, or even five minutes after that particular thing happened.

The great mystic Cynthia Bourgeault reveals the process of this simple mystery when she writes, "By the power of the divine indwelling within me, I unconditionally embrace the moment, no matter its physical or psychological content."

Every time I sit with the hurt, I let it hit me as hard as it can until it's drained of its power, and each time, the only thing left is love.

In these unguarded and open spaces with love and light, we become the fulfillment of Hafiz's great wish when he said, "I wish I could show you when you are lonely or in darkness the astonishing light of your own being." In these undefended moments, we must squint at the light of our own being, because if we turn too quickly we will be blinded by the infinite light of God.

Someone you truly counted on didn't show up for you when you needed them the most.

Someone you love more than anyone else in the world absolutely crushed you with their words.

Someone you thought would be next to you supporting you, building with you, and fighting for you not only left, but is now sitting around tables with other people you know bad mouthing you, and it hurts.

Or maybe the issue is not people, its circumstances.

You are not where you thought you would be vocationally at this point in your life, and a part of you feels shame about that.

Your business, your church, your brand, your thing has not gone the way you thought it was going to go, and you're frustrated, and it's taking away the joy you had when it started.

You feel like you're supposed to be further than where you are and it hurts to think about, and it can become paralyzing at times trying to have the energy to keep going.

The people who hurt us, disappoint us, or betray us will stay with us if we don't forgive them. The circumstances that frustrate us, upset us, or discourage us remain in us if we can't accept them. The boundaries that limit us, hinder us, and prevent us from owning our voice and embracing our adventure will remain in power if we don't transcend them.

So how can we move through our life and relationships beyond the barriers of resentment and frustration?

Well,
You don't fight something you've already forgiven.
You don't get angry at something you've already accepted.
You don't linger with anything you've already let go of.

+ + +

About three years into the life of Imagine, I had a painful falling out with a person from the small group of people that we started the church with. This was the closest friend I made after moving back to Honolulu, and my most trusted co-laborer in the church since it began. This was a person who my wife and I welcomed into our life, who would sleep in our home, who would dream with us for the future, and who, just months before our relationship ended, wrote my wife and I a card thanking us for everything we did for him, even saying that we were like family to him.

I loved this guy.

And even though there were challenges in the relationship along the way, after one accidentally sent text message by me with hurtful words on it (don't ever do that!), a long and painful conversation, five weeks of waiting to hear back from him, he decided he wanted nothing to do with the church or with us any more.

This is the moment where a personal hit actually feels like a cosmic punch to the gut.

Immediately after our last conversation, I went to a secret spot in the mountains here in Honolulu and spent time in silence, shed some tears, and performed a ritual for letting go. I forgave him for any hurt I felt he did to me, let go of any expectations I had, and accepted the circumstances of my life for exactly what they were in the moment.

After I did that, I felt no resistance, no frustration, and no anger. I still felt the pain from the wound itself, but there was no frustration with the pain, because there wasn't any non-acceptance of the pain.

You can be free from any resistance to pain, while still feeling the reality of pain.

Yes, I had forgiven him for what he did, but it was also bigger than him.

Here's the thing.

It's always bigger than the person.

It's the person, but it's actually a pattern.

It's the pattern through them, but it's actually a pattern beyond them in life itself.

Here is what I mean.

Whenever a person does something, it is never a completely isolated act, it is always a particular instantiation of a pattern that exists in their life. So, when a situation arises where you need to forgive, you're not just forgiving the person for what they did, you're forgiving them for the larger pattern they have.

And to extend that even further, it's not just a pattern for them, it's a pattern in life.

It's not just forgiving them for turning their back when you opened your heart and gave them everything you had, it's accepting that we live in a world where you can give everything you have to someone and they will still end up walking away.

It's not just forgiving him for leaving when he was the one I counted on the most, it's accepting that sometimes the people you count on are not going to stick around and are eventually going to leave.

It's not just forgiving him for hurting me, it's forgiving reality itself for a being a place where I can get hurt.

It's not just the person, it's the pattern.

In each moment of your life when you are facing a person who needs to be forgiven or circumstances that needs to be accepted, the particular is always an open door the universal.

You wrestle with forgiving the person in flesh and blood because of what they did, but you are really wrestling with life itself for what it is. You're frustrated because specific circumstances have not gone the way you wanted, but you are really struggling with the expectations you had on how life is supposed to work. You're angry at how things went for you when you're really having a hard time accepting life for how it goes.

It's not only forgiving the pain another person inflicted, it's accepting the world that is inevitably going to cause you pain.

It's not just accepting that this person is indifferent to your work, it's accepting that not everyone is going to care about what you're doing.

It's not just allowing that person to make self destructive decisions after all of the guidance you gave them, it's accepting that some people are going to make bad decisions no matter what you say or how much you care.

It has to begin with, "How can I forgive them and accept what they've done? But it needs to eventually extend to, "How can I forgive reality for being like this, and accept the world for what it is?"

When you zoom in, you're forgiving the person for what they did, but when you zoom out, what you're really doing is forgiving the pattern in this universe.

It's as if the particular moment provides a ladder from the concrete person all the way up to the cosmic pattern. Where you can discover that real freedom is not whether or not you can forgive it down here, its whether or not you can accept it up there.

Real freedom comes not from forgiving the concrete person, it comes from accepting the cosmic pattern.

Which is why the scientist and theologian Ilia Delio says, "Heaven unfolds when we see things for what they are, not what we think they should be, and when we love others for who they are, and not what we expect them to be."

Our struggle with the particular always comes out of our inability accept the universal.

+ + +

In Matthew 18, we encounter an interesting conversation between Jesus and Peter. The text says, "Then Peter came to Jesus and asked, 'Lord, how many times shall I forgive my brother or sister who sins against me? Up to seven times?' Jesus answered, not seven times, but seventy-seven times."

Then immediately after this exchange, Jesus proceeds to tell a compelling story that is broadly about mercy and forgiveness.

Now, despite all of the social and cultural details that would open this story up further, there is a very simple, but radical reading of this text. This is not about a math equation that helps us figure out how many different times we are supposed to forgive individuals when they betray us, make mistakes, or cause us pain.

This about a more universal posture of forgiveness and unconditional embrace of life itself.

At its most simple and radical level, Jesus is inviting human beings to forgive reality for being what it is—flawed, imperfect, broken, and probably not what you expected it to be. This is about accepting reality for what it is, forgiving reality for what it is not, and letting go of the need for anything to be different than it is right now in order for you to be able to experience the grace and peace Christ offers.

It is not primarily about choosing to forgive individuals when they hurt us, it is actually about choosing to express to them the universal forgiveness you have already offered to the world.

We accept the pain they caused, let go of the need for them to be different than they are, and forgive them of their hurt, because we have already accepted pain as a part of life, we have already let go of the need for the world to be different, and we have already forgiven the world for being a place where pain exists.

When you forgive it at the universal, it no longer bothers you in the particular.

When you accept it on the cosmic map, it no longer rules over you in the concrete moment.

When you see the pattern, it no longer surprises you at the personal.

When you wrestle with it, fight with it, and finally submit to it as a whole, you are able to allow it, accept it, and be okay with it as a part.

It's not just personal, it's a pattern.

It's not just concrete, it's cosmic.

And if we learn how to forgive it, accept it, and allow it up there, we will always be free from it down here.

MORE MUSHROOMS AND THE MOST IMPORTANT MOMENT OF MY LIFE

A few nights after New Year's Eve in 2003, I thought I that might die.

Or at least need to be checked into a psychiatric unit, put in a straight jacket, and be under professional medical watch for a while.

I knew things were about to get bad.

At about midnight on that defining night, I had eaten more mushrooms than I had ever eaten, I was with my best friend Squirrel (I should have known it would go bad), and within an hour, I was tiptoeing on the edge of darkness, sanity, and what felt like death.

(I told you I would get back to this moment.)

The world was melting around me, I was sitting in a chair flexing every muscle I had, desperately trying to fight off what was happening to me. If I stopped fighting and resisting, I felt like

I would slowly begin to collapse like a folding chair onto the ground.

I could feel darkness starting to envelop my entire being, I could feel the weight of everything wrong with the world pressing down on my shoulders and infiltrating my mind, and I turned to my friend sitting on my bed, looked into his beady little eyes and said,

"I don't feel right."

And without any hesitation or breaking of eye contact, with a terrifying look on his face, he looked into my soul and said, "Me neither."

That was not what I was hoping to hear.

I was tripping.

I was scared.

I was overwhelmed.

I thought that I might die.

I was scared to death and overwhelmed, and I was only one hour into what is normally a four to six hour experience.

As I was internally panicking, I started to tell my friend I needed to go to the hospital. I looked at him and without any fear of consequences said,

"I need to go to the hospital, I need to be strapped to a bed, and I need to be under the watch and care of a professional. I don't care if I get arrested, I don't care if my parents find out, I don't care about any of that. I'm going."

And with all of the sensitivity, empathy and wisdom another eighteen year old could muster up in this traumatic of an event, my friend looked back at me and immediately said,

"Nah man."

The kind of genius response that should have landed him a spot on Oprah's Super Soul Sunday.

But what happened next was surprising. In the midst of an existential break down, a melting reality, and a racing mind, something deep within me said, "Call Christine."

I kept hearing that.

"Call Christine." "Call Christine."

So, I called Christine (my girlfriend I had just rekindled my love with after she came back from college in Hawaii for Christmas) and said, "Im with Squirrel. I'm tripping, I'm not well. I'm coming over."

She responded the way a normal person would respond to this call at one in the morning.

"Kevin, it's one in the morning, my parents are home, they will kill me if you guys come over." (Looking back, it's hilarious to think what my wife's innocent Vietnamese parents would think if they came into her room and saw two young white kids freaking out on mushrooms!)

I responded like a maniac by repeating the phrase, 'I can't hear this right now. I can't hear this right now. I can't hear this right now. We're coming over!"

Despite some reasonable resistance, she finally said okay. So I called another friend to come pick us up and give us a ride (I may have threatened him a little) to her house, and as I slumped in the front seat, too afraid to look out the window, little did I know I was on a ride to a brand new future.

After we got to her place and Christine stopped shaking her head and looking at me like I was crazy (which is understandable), and the house finally stopped shaking, I started to calm down. Don't get me wrong, I was still one hundred percent tripping on mushrooms, it was just that I was calm, I felt present again and I was no longer resisting.

And after all three of us talked for a while in her dimly lit room only illuminated by a couple candles and her glow in the dark stars on the ceiling, Christine drifted off to sleep, and Squirrel remained quiet. I lied down in the bed for the next couple of hours, not knowing I would eventually get up as an entirely new person.

As I lied there after I settled down, I was completely open, my heart was unguarded, and as I allowed my whole being to be in a state of pure vulnerability and receptivity, I could spiritually and almost physically feel light being fused into my entire being.

Unconditional love was giving itself to me fully and freely.

I sensed pure affirmation, a universal "yes" being spoken over my life, and the clarity to see that in my most fragile state when I had nothing to offer or give, the presence of love becomes everything I am.

It was the validation of a father, the warmth of a mother, the touch of a healer, the closeness of a friend, the embrace of a lover, and the unmatched power of creation becoming personal and giving birth to something within me.

It was the Source itself, the Reality of the possibility I was searching for here with me, in me, flowing through me, and without a shadow of a doubt, totally for me.

I experienced that the electricity that charges the universe is also the light of my life, the glue that holds together all things is also the grace that holds me, and the love that is the deepest dimension of life, is also the depth of who I am.

I knew exactly what happened—I experienced God.

Now, here is what is so interesting about this experience.

There were no Bible verses.

No friend inviting me to youth group (I didn't even know those existed).

No sinner's prayer.

Just the immediate experience of the divine.

My primary experience of the Spirit was pure union with God, fusion with light, and a true falling into love.

When I got up from that bed a couple hours later, I was a different person.

With my limited religious language or limited amount of spiritual concepts available to me, immediately after that experience I said to myself,

"This was a re-birth."

I could not conceptualize everything that happened, and I still can't, but I did know I was as radically born again as a human being can possibly be, and I didn't even know that was a thing.

Even on the car ride home in the glowing wake of this experience, I remember thinking to myself, "Its not that I am having different thoughts about life (although I was), it is that the very "I" that is having those thoughts is a completely different thing."

I did not know at the time that what I was describing was the transformation of consciousness itself. It wasn't, "I am now having new thoughts about life, it was the fundamental "I" that is having those thoughts has actually been made new.

This was not just a re-thinking of concepts, it was the rewiring of my consciousness itself.

Without any guidance from an elder, without any validation from a religious leader, without the presence of any external authority being able to confirm what I had experienced,

I knew.

I knew exactly what happened.

I did not seek nor need any validation, confirmation, or verification from any external authority because the truth of what happened was being validated, confirmed, and verified by the very Source of life itself.

So, when Shane Hipps writes, "[Jesus] came to introduce us to the most easily forgotten and often overlooked miracle of all—our existence and the heaven hidden within it." I knew the introduction had been made.

+ + +

To conclude this story, and to take it even one step further, (I know what you're thinking: There's more?) there is one more significant thing happened when I got home.

When I got home it was about five in the morning. My parents (who had picked us up) went back to bed, and Squirrel and I decided to go outside and smoke a blunt in the back of my brother's truck as a way to mark the experience I just had.

While we were smoking and I was explaining to my friend what just happened to me, there was one impossibly bright star in the sky staring down at us, almost like the universe itself was giving me a wink. When we were done, I went into my room and had this inner dialogue and experience that I will never forget.

I was laying in my bed, Squirrel was laying on the floor, and I had this internal conversation.

"I'm thirsty."

"But I'm too comfortable and lazy to get up and some water for myself."

"I should ask Squirrel to get it for me. He's my friend. He will go get me water if I ask him."

"But do you need water?

No.

Then why would you ask somebody else to get you what you don't need?"

"Yeah. I'm good."

And in that moment of acknowledging that I didn't need water to be at peace, which was at a deeper level, the inner recognition that I did not need anything else outside of God to be okay, my inner dialogue stopped, I rested in the wholeness of God and myself, and closed my eyes.

And in that exact instant, seemingly out of nowhere, and in a fashion that would be nothing short of a miracle, Squirrel turned around and looked at me and asked,

"Do you want me to get you some water?"

I was in shock.

I received that as this final confirmation from the presence of God saying, "Everything that just happened was real, trust what you know and what you see, have faith I am in you and seeing with you."

I went to sleep and my life was never the same.

+ + +

My life totally changed the next few years, and as I kept growing and evolving, I would often reflect on why my initial encounter with Christ was so immediately transformative, and why my experience of God so naturally became a constant flow with God.

And I have some thoughts on why.

So let's turn to the apostle Paul and some of the great mystics to makes some sense of why my experience was as unique as it was.

In a letter to the Ephesians, Paul mentions that "in regard to your former way of life, to put off your old self…and to put on the new self."

One of the most prominent mystics from the West, Meister Eckhart said, "God is not found in the soul by adding anything, but by a process of subtraction."

Rumi said, "Your task is not to seek for love, but merely to seek and find all the barriers within yourself that you have built against it."

Each voice is saying that the journey is not travel the ends of the earth in order to finally find God, the journey is to travel to the depths of your own inner life in order to remove everything that is getting in the way of the love that is eternally here.

Now it makes sense to me why that spontaneous awakening moment was so immediate and powerful.

I had already dis-identified with my ego in such a radical way.

I had already died to the false self that hustled for its worth outside of God.

I had already recognized my illusions for what they were.

My life had become a giant runway for Spirit.

When I met God, I was not a good person (despite how much my mom justified my behavior publicly in order to avoid shame).

Sorry mom.

Morality, trying hard, being good, or any form earning the right to be seen and loved by God had nothing to do with my experience. When it comes to deep transformation, it is not about whether or not you are good or bad, it's about whether you are
open or closed,
receptive or clinging,
unguarded or defensive.

Letting go of my illusions cleared out space for my freedom. Already naming my wounds opened up the space where I actually needed the healing power of love. Recognizing my ego and all of the ways my separate self attempted to get its needs met outside of God swung open the doors in my heart to welcome and take in the love and presence of God.

What happened to my life after this night is nothing short of a miracle, which is why you need to keep reading on.

JESUS WAS FREE

Most people commonly think of Jesus as a person who helps set people free, but what we don't think about as naturally is the fact that Jesus Himself was free. We think of Jesus as someone who frees people, but not Jesus as a free person. Jesus was born out of this world not only to lead humanity into freedom, but to show us what it looks like to lead humanity freely.

When we arrive at the end of John 6, Jesus' ministry is filled with momentum.

Jesus just multiplied fish and bread and miraculously fed a large group of people. Jesus performed what would eventually become one of the most famous miracles in human history, and the Scriptures report that the people were searching for him, following him, calling him a prophet, and were trying to force him to become king!

This is Jesus' moment.

This is where things are supposed to take off.

If this was our culture, then the next logical move would be a book deal, a stadium tour, and merch! (I only had two of these for this book, so please stop judging me.)

And then right in the midst of this moment, Jesus offers a challenging teaching, and many of the people completely change their posture toward him and leave.

John 6:66 says, "From this time, many of the disciples turned back and no longer followed him."

The people who were moving toward him are now moving away from him, the people who were celebrating him are now criticizing him, and the people who were ready to crown him king are now nowhere to be found. And after this begins to happen, Jesus turns to one of his closest comrades Peter, and essentially says, "You can leave too if you want." And Peter responds by communicating "This is real, where else am I going to go (my translation)?"

Jesus' response is him saying, I am not going to allow the response of others to prevent me from living my truth. I am not going to allow the expectations of others to prevent me from speaking my truth. And I am not going to betray my own integrity, transgress any of my own boundaries, or try to sway or manipulate anyone to stay around.

Jesus chooses authenticity over attraction.

Jesus chooses what's real over what's right now.

And ultimately Jesus shows us that value is something that is given by us, not given to us.

Jesus' day to day life puts on display what a life of liberated love looks like. You will not come across one occurrence of Jesus chasing someone down, trying to win them over, and trying to manipulate their journey in any way out of his own agenda to have more people around him (which pastors and leaders can be tempted to do).

Not one time do you see Jesus close his heart, create distance, withhold himself, write people off, or move into any passive aggressive behavior toward someone who hurt or offended him (which pastors and leaders are also tempted to do).

Jesus doesn't just set us free, he shows us what it looks like to be free

His life shows us that there is a way to live out of that wide open space of love without being destroyed by the responses of anyone else. The way he engages with people up until the very end of his life lights up a path where, as Brueggemann said, we can be "deeply concerned for, and utterly free from other people."

You can be concerned for others without being governed by them, you can love others while being liberated from them, you can care for others without being controlled by them.

Jesus was free to love with his whole life,

Which is why the real question becomes, how can we be free to love with ours as well?

+ + +

One thing most people will never fully grasp is the maddening experience of being a pastor.

Being a pastor means you have chosen a vocation that has built into it almost every single challenging thing that most human beings spend their entire lives avoiding. And like any other vocational path, unless you do this, you have no idea what it's really like.

The struggles you go through, the invisible burdens you carry, that deep unconscious pressure you can feel, and that hidden yet powerful internal voice of the ego that keeps saying the same thing over and over—you're not doing enough.

What you do as a pastor, and especially as a church planter, is a collision of all of the hardest parts of many of the most challenging endeavors. The resilience of the start up or small business owner, the constant content requirement of the freelancer, creative or artist. The relational complexity and the consistent bearing witness to suffering faced by the therapist, and of course, the unconscious placing of yourself into a family system like dynamic where everyone gets to play out their dramatic childhood narratives through you and with you.

Who wants to sign up?

Here's a few examples of the weird or painful things I've experienced leading Imagine over the years.

I've had a pastor from another church show up to our Good Friday event and whisper into the ear of someone in our church that he's here to see if this was a cult. (Nothing says let's remember the crucifixion like being suspected of being a cult leader.)

Another pastor from a different church intentionally sat down two young men in our church to make sure they were okay because he was worried about them since they were a part of our church (He must have been friends with the first guy.)

I heard a person tell me that their boyfriend, who came to Imagine a few times, believes all I do is offer people inspirational fluff. (Good thing I spent all that time preparing those sermons!)

I've had multiple people I cared for deeply leave the church and publicly criticize me and attack my character. (Those ones just hurt.)

I've had people I loved and welcomed into my home turn on me like you couldn't imagine, I've heard that someone said I follow the devil's plan because of how we welcome LGBTQ people, I've had the people I've counted on the most betray me and break my heart, and that doesn't even cover the constant and casual flow of people in and out of your life that you are choosing to keep showing up for.

Again, who wants to sign up!?

But, here is why I share these experiences.

I've had many reasons to shut down parts of my heart, close off parts of my life, withhold parts of my love, and to decide that a life of Christ-shaped love is, in the end, not worth it. But Jesus' life reveals something deeply true about our relationships.

The feedback of other people says nothing about the faithfulness of God.

This is why it's all the small stuff with Jesus in the gospels that means the most to me as a pastor.

When John 6:66 says, "From this time many of his disciples turned back and no longer followed him."

What I see here are people admiring Jesus, that they want to be close to him, that they're even ready to crown him king. But what I also see is that when Jesus speaks another dimension of truth, many of these same people just walk away.

We can glance at this and not even recognize it, but when you have had people who have once exclaimed their support for you eventually walk away from you, you know how hard it is.

Or in Matthew 19:22 "When the young man heard this, he went away sad, because he had great wealth."

Jesus shows this young man what is getting in the way of his own freedom, and right when he's close to the threshold of the new, he returns to the old, refuses to see differently, and he walks away.

Someone asks you for guidance, but lying within this relationship at all times is the ever present possibility that you will finally speak a depth of truth that they will not be ready to embrace, and as a result, choose to exclude you from their life.

This is just a part of it.

And in Mark 8:32, "He spoke plainly about this, and Peter took him aside and began to rebuke him."

Right after Peter tells Jesus He believes he is the messiah, Jesus essentially says yes, but not like how you think I'm supposed to be, and not in the way your ego needs to me to be. And immediately after, Peter rebukes him in front of all of their friends.

This is the inevitability of disappointing people you care about. Jesus, as the full embodiment of truth and love was still a disappointment to the people following him.

No matter what people thought, no matter what people said, no matter how other people responded to him, Jesus puts on display a life that is lived in complete authenticity and truth. And we can live this way too.

+ + +

We need to learn the art of being faithful to people yet free from them.

It is both a humble and liberating thing to realize that our lives are simply offerings. We are not saviors, we cannot fix people, and we have absolutely no control over any decisions other people make. And Jesus shows us is that it is in us fully accepting these realities, while still choosing to give our lives faithfully to people that real freedom lies.

Whenever we hear someone speak of the possibility of a more liberated path, it isn't enough to know why it's important to make changes to receive it. It isn't even enough to have the clarity on what it is, or to get inspired to commit to the path itself, what is needed is to gain clarity on the how.

How do we become more free, and how can we live with the authenticity and love Jesus embodied?

Too often spiritual leaders communicate why we need something and what we need, while at the same time leaving out the most practical part of the path—which is the how. (My suspicion is that they don't always know the answer themselves). So, as we imagine a path where we can keep our heart space open and our interactions with others as free as Jesus' were, let's look at a few ways that show us how it is possible to follow this path.

We can love people and liberate them at the same time.

The only way to love another person is to completely liberate them, which is actually you being liberated from them. To be even more clear, being liberated from another person means to unconditionally let go of the need for anything from them.

Anything.
I really mean anything.
And anything means everything.

It means to completely surrender any and all expectations on people. It means accepting that you do not have any control over how others are going to respond to you, your love, or whatever you're trying to give them. It means learning that the response of someone else says nothing about the essence of who you are.

By the way, this is just another way talking about the essential need for real differentiation. What they do with what you give cannot add or take away anything essential from who you are.

How they respond to what you create says nothing about the always present peace that is available to you. How many people showed up to participate in the event you were throwing subtracts nothing from the value of the offering you gave, or more importantly from the inherent value you have.

What does what they are doing have anything to do with your joy, your peace, and your freedom? What do you think you need from others in order to feel good about your love for and commitment to them?

Why do we have a hard time just letting other people be?

Think about how Jesus relates to the people around him. The ones who doubt him are still the ones close to him. The one who would eventually betray him was still welcomed by Jesus throughout his life. The one who would publicly deny him was one of the people Jesus committed to and cared for the most. Even when people saw Jesus after the resurrection, the Scriptures say that some who were close to him still doubted. And yet he still was as committed to them as possible.

Jesus lives out the beautiful path of absolute love for and radical release from.

Perhaps it's more accurate to say that in order to love people we need to be liberated from them.

+ + +

It's not about you.

A lot of people who are in the healing business, especially pastors, have a hard time letting go of expectations and allowing people to simply be. It's too easy to believe people's behavior or decisions is a reflection of your own quality of work, which then affects how you feel about your value.

Take a second to allow that last sentence to sink in.

At an unconscious level, people do not feel the freedom to love someone deeply and then just allow them to be, because too much of their own belief about the value of their offering is tied to the decisions other people make after they receive their offering.

If this person were pastoring starts to wake up, starts to demonstrate change, starts to show more commitment to Jesus or to the church, then we can feel good.

But if another person, who we have spent the exact same amount of time with, keeps making self-destructive decisions, starts to create distance, leaves the church, or goes back to some of their old ways, then we will feel bad because deep down we believe it is somehow our fault or responsibility.

Like I said, it's not about you.

It's about them.
It's their life.
It's their path.

You are just a guide.

Only they can make decisions that have the power to shape their own life. You're a pastor, a guide, a teacher, a friend, a support, and you can do all of that wholeheartedly without personalizing any decision other people make or allowing those decisions to alter your own center in Christ.

+ + +

There is a difference between hope and expectations.

Talking to people about the radical letting go of all expectations on others will usually create some resistance within them, which will then naturally lead to some push back.

I get it. But I still mean it.

The enlightened path has no expectations.

And to add to that, this path knows there is a difference between hope and expectations.

Hope says, I really want this for you.

Expectations say, I really want this for you, and I won't be okay if you don't do it.

Hope says, I believe in you and am going to give my time, energy, and love in order to help you live into this new thing.

Expectations say, I am going to give my time, energy, and love in order to help you live into this new thing, and if you don't follow all the way through, I am going to be bothered, irritated, or hurt.

Hope says I will welcome you into my life, but no matter what you choose or how you respond, I am going to be fine because I am free from you.

Expectations say, I will welcome you into my life, but if you don't appreciate me, show gratitude, come through for me, or do whatever my ego needs you to do, I'm going to remain hurt, disappointed, angry or resentful.

Hope is the power that enables you to work for the freedom in this world while remaining free yourself.

+ + +

Forgiveness, acceptance, and letting go are everything.

The mystic knows that deep spirituality and freedom are always about forgiveness, acceptance, and letting go. And if you truly long to be a person who can live with the same kind of authenticity as Jesus, you need to get really, really, really good at all three of these.

Forgiveness is not one thing that you place alongside of everything else, it is the thing that flows through and holds together everything else.

While we are walking this impossible path of loving like Jesus, the problem is not that some people are never going to show you the appreciation you deserve, the problem is that you haven't let go of the need to be appreciated by others in order to feel good about your offering.

The problem is not that other people might betray you when you open yourself up to love, the problem is that you have not accepted that in order to love in this world, you have to embrace the possibility of betrayal.

The problem is not that things didn't go the way you planned, the problem is that you cannot let go of the way you thought thing were supposed to be, and thus, remain unable to embrace where things are.

We are always forgiving people.

We are always accepting unwanted circumstances.

We are always letting go of expectations on people and the illusions we still carry around about how life is supposed to be.

+ + +

Love never imposes, it always invites.

The first part of that sentence I get from the great living mystic, James Finley. The second part I added.

Only the non-essential, superficial, and the shallow has to impose itself on others. The freedom of Jesus to keep his heart space wide open to give, while also letting people go, be in process, while being consistently misunderstood and not appreciated is truly phenomenal.

After starting Imagine and pastoring, leading, and creating for seven years, I have never burnt out, I hold no grudges, I have not shut down my heart, I have not fallen into withholding in any way, and I am more filled with joy than I even knew was possible when I began.

(This does not mean I have not failed, made mistakes, or hurt people. I have many times.)

This is only possible through
acceptance,
letting go,
and forgiveness.

There is so much of pastoring, organizational leadership, and leading in general I am terrible at. But living in a constant flow of acceptance, letting go, and forgiveness is what has allowed me to do what I do without losing my own joy.

If you desire to be a person who is as free as Jesus was to pour himself out for the sake of the world, while remaining free in the process, these three need to become some of your closest companions, your most trusted friends, and your most reliable guides.

IDOLS, HEROES, AND GURUS

One of the greatest gifts of my spiritual journey was being able to meet, be close to, and be disappointed by virtually every single one of my idols.

When I was a freshman in High School playing varsity basketball, I not only became teammates with some of my idols, I became close friends with them. At fifteen, this was a dream come true. It felt like a magical time in my life, forming a powerful bond on the court, and staying close off the court by smoking weed together everyday, hanging out all the time, and going to parties.

These eighteen year old "gods," who just one year before, I was watching in absolute awe of from the sideline while I was in eighth grade, were now picking me up for school, driving me to every party, and passing me the ball at three point line on a fast break.

But eventually my heroes would become human, these gods would crash from the heavens to earth, and my idols would shatter.

After my freshman year, I started drifting apart from the one guy I looked up to the most. I was heartbroken as his flaws and imperfections started to surface for me. It wasn't any one thing that opened my eyes, just a litany of small things that exposed the humanity within him that a part of me did not want to see.

Isn't it strange how the humanity and flaws of another person can change how we feel toward them?

He got in trouble in college and kicked off his team, I started to be better than he was in basketball (you can't be more powerful than your hero), and we got into some serious arguing one day that almost led to a fight. And I just began to realize he was self-centered, manipulative, and I did not like being around him anymore.

His mystique was gone, his power was stripped, and I accepted he wasn't the god I needed him to be.

He was human, and for some reason, that hurt for me to realize at that age.

It is a strange occurrence that the flaws, imperfections, and humanity of another person can somehow feel like a disappointment to us. It is as if we needed more from them than they could offer.

And that's the problem.

Unexpectedly at the time, but obviously now as I look back, this cycle of idolization, personal connection, and impending disappointment kept going.

My basketball heroes became my peers, and when I was around them as people, I was unimpressed. After I started rapping at sixteen, I would be in cyphers with underground stars at house parties, or in the studio with West Coast legends (who will remain nameless), and every single time, I would be confronted with the inevitable moment where I saw my heroes as the imperfect, insecure, and fragile human beings they were. And every single time I was disappointed. This became an inescapable cycle.

And again, they weren't the problem, my expectations on them and what I needed them to be was the real problem.

During this season of my life, and in the midst of these cycles, I noticed something else happening within me. Whenever I would lose a hero, I would be more in touch with my own heroic possibilities. Whenever the power of my false god would be stripped, I would realize more of how powerful I was. It was as if seeing the weakness in them somehow liberated the eyes of my heart to see more strength in myself.

Every time I would lose one of my heroes, I would gain more of my voice.

+ + +

It's 2015 and two and a half years after I moved back to Hawaii, and after going through those first wonderful and challenging two years of starting a church, I was going to California for five days for a time of rest and inspiration.

My wife had gotten me tickets to go to an event with Richard Rohr. And as I landed at LAX and drove to Orange County, I actually said out loud to myself with a subtle smile on my face,

"I am here to watch my heroes become human, and to watch my idols crash to the ground."

When I said that, it wasn't a negative assessment of Rohr at all, it was the acknowledgment of the pattern within me and the structure of my ego I had recognized fifteen years earlier. At this point, he was one of the only people left in the world at the time who still had any degree of that old, looking up to the senior on the basketball team, naïve, kind of mystique left for me—even though by now in my life, I had let go of the need for anyone to be that.

So, at this point in my life, I no longer felt the same kind of disappointment when this happened, it was just a kind of ritual my distant ego would go through as I would calmly observe.

Rohr was the first person I read, at age twenty-three, who ever named the experience in life I knew I had with God. And he powerfully represented a status quo challenging and mystical depth as a follower of Jesus that I resonated with.

I did not need gods anymore, but I was thankful to have him as a guide.

As I was going to this event, it was almost like a religious pilgrimage, a death ritual my ego would go through in order to keep going deeper into owning my own voice.

Let's be honest for a second.

A lot of us have this fantasy of going to a Richard Rohr event (or whoever you look up to), having them single you out, desire to befriend you, tell you that everything you ever thought you were capable of is true, and maybe even bring you up in front of everyone else and tell them the ultimate truth—that in fact, you are the one.

(I'm sure my ego is not the only one with that kind of an imagination!)

And maybe not the last part about being the one.

But kind of.

But there is something within these fantasies that is critical to pay attention to. The energy surging though the fantasies is this deep thing within us that longs for some distant, more powerful, more evolved, and special figure to find us and give us something we believe we need to be fully ourselves.

So, here's the question:

What do we ultimately desire from these fantasy like scenarios with our idols and would be gurus?

We want them to tell us that everything we ever believed we were capable of is true.

We want them to give us the permission to be everything we dream of being.

We want them to befriend us and offer to personally mentor us and be with us.

Okay, well, what is all of that anyway?

Recognition.
Affirmation.
Validation.
Permission.
Connection.

This is why having idols and gurus can become a massive obstacle to us knowing our own voice, and embracing the unique adventure of our own path. When we look to these seemingly special people, we want affirmation we don't need, validation they can't give us, and permission they don't have the authorization to offer us.

We keep looking to others to tell us what, at a deeper level, we already know is true about us. We are seeking out from those we perceive as more powerful than us what the Spirit can give to us directly.

The recognition of the uniqueness of who we are.

The validation of our inherent value as human beings.

The permission to create, make, love, and build for a better world.

Whatever you imagine and long for from that guru, or leader, or speaker, to affirm within you is probably already true about you. It seems like we have a hard time trusting our own power unless it is affirmed by someone who is in power.

+ + +

There are no those people.

Too many of us live with this unconscious and disempowered idea that there are those people—and that they are the ones who get to do creative, innovative, and interesting things. Only those people get to start companies, write books, throw cool events, and get to be a part of exciting organizations who are working for change in this world. Only those people get to live their dream, use their voice, and live so freely.

This is why I will say it again. There are no those people.

Those people are you if you live with courage.

Those people are you if you take that risk.

Those people are you if you realize how powerful you are.

Idols crashing, heroes becoming human, gods falling to the earth, and gurus being de-mystified are all essential parts of the exciting path of discovering your own voice and walking your unique path in this world.

When the imperfection of our idols are exposed, the power within ourselves is revealed.

As long as we keep projecting all of the magic over there with them, we are never going to recognize all of the magic right here with us. And as long as we keep looking to what we perceive as powerful people to authorize our voice from the outside, we will tragically miss out on the authorizing presence of the Spirit of God that is dwelling on the inside.

There are no those people.

+ + +

Back to my trip and the Rohr event.

It was a fantastic time. Father Rohr is brilliant, a person of integrity and alignment, and I would argue is at the leading edge of culture and consciousness in the West. But despite the profundity shared during the event—based on the ego pattern I described before about idols—the biggest thing I took away was not something I heard from the outside, it was something more that emerged on the inside.

This is a part of what I wrote late at night on the plane ride back home to Hawaii after the event.

"In the end…what do I leave with? Do I leave with this electricity of inspiration flowing in me that pumps me up to come back and explode with new life, new resolves, new fortitude?! No. Do I leave with this deep soulful thought that says,"I have sat at the feet of the great sages and their presence was felt, and powerful, and transcendent in and of itself, and it was everything I dreamed it would be and more?" No. Do I leave with the fundamental new insight about what is going to open up the new, broader, more beautiful, more expansive future of the faith and of the world? No. Well if not any of those things, then what is the most valuable thing I leave with from this trip and experience? I leave with even more of an acceptance of the power within my voice. I leave with this deep sense of affirmation (from the gaze of God) that I was on the right path all along. I leave with even more of a desire to create, not because of how it will build my brand, but because of how it can build the future. I leave knowing and being grounded in the reality that this is my time to give everything I have…"

So, in the end, when our idols have crashed, when our gurus have failed us, when our gods have fallen from the heavens, and our heroes have become human, what we are left with is just us.

And if you can dare to see the sacred gift and responsibility of what that truly means, you will know that is a good thing.

THE THING AFTER
THE THING

A lot of people know about the idea of the thing behind the thing.

During a conversation, there is the thing (what we're talking about), and then there is the thing behind the thing (what we are really talking about).

Or, I am angry about the comment they just said to me (the thing). But I am actually embarrassed, and this embarrassment triggers this deeper insecurity I have about feeling humiliated in front of others, and how I will be exposed in the process (the thing behind the thing).

Or, you're frustrated with the flow of the leadership team you're a part of (that's the thing), but as we keep talking, the truth is you actually felt left out because you weren't included in an excursion, and you have a hard time admitting that you were hurt (that's the thing behind thing).

See how that works?

We spend so much time and energy on the thing, when the real work is a few steps deeper with the thing behind the thing.

If you can see the inner working of the thing behind the thing in real time, it creates a great sense of clarity when you're trying to get a handle on what is happening within you. The quicker you can feel the energy of the thing behind the thing, the faster you are able to settle into wisdom.

But there is also the thing after the thing.

The thing after the thing gets in the way of so much of what we want in life. Our inability to accept the thing after the thing is a major barrier to our capacity to experience the wholeness we desire.

While people spend so much time avoiding, denying, or wrestling with the thing, it's really the thing after the thing that they're scared of.

A couple years ago, my friend Larry and I were leading people through an experience called Flow at a co-working space around our neighborhood. We taught people about the calling on humanity to be culture makers, how co-creating the world is at the center of our vocational identity, and how having a hopeful vision of the future enables meaningful action in the present. Through this group, we were going to launch a new cultural initiative for the benefit of our community.

After some of the initial ideas were introduced to people, we had a discussion one night about what gets in the way of us innovating, creating, and risking more freely. And while the conversation did not go the direction we anticipated, the mutual discovery in the room was exactly what we all needed to see.

And the clarity that came from that conversation was that the invisible ground beneath the discussion about creating was our insecure relationship with our inherent value.

(By the way, it's somehow always about value.)

In a room filled with high level project managers, financial advisors, freelancers, photographers, marketing strategists, and content creators, we ended up talking about our struggle to trust our inherent value, and why we allow so many nonessential things to become such a threat to it.

As each person shared about personal barriers to their own creative life, and some of the fears attached to those barriers, we realized there was a universal pattern within the personal stories.

The pattern was structured like this:

This is my fear.

This is what it would mean if it was actualized.

And ultimately, this is the negative thing this materialization of my fear would say about who I am and my value.

This universal pattern would sound slightly different depending on the personal story, but beneath the surface it was the same pattern, and each time had the same ultimate end result. What they were really afraid of, the thing that was really after everything else, was that somehow their fear coming true meant that they were less valuable.

My thing doesn't work.

I fail.

Or I am humiliated.

Or I get criticized.

And somehow, this takes away from the substance of who I am.

So, it plays out in our imaginations like this.

If I try and start this new thing, I might fail (that's the thing).

If I fail, people will know, and if they know, they won't respect or admire me anymore.

If people don't admire me, this means I'm less valuable (that's the thing after the thing).

If I create a gallery of my own work or throw this event, people might not come. If people don't come, I will be humiliated and others will think I don't have what it takes to make a living as an artist. If people don't believe in me or my work, this means I'm less valuable

Each person. Different stories. Same structure. Always about value.

The problem is not the thing, it's the thing after the thing that you cannot accept that is the real problem.

It's not that you're scared of trying, its that you still believe that if you try your hardest and it doesn't work out, it takes away value from you.

It's not that you're worried about disappointing people you respect if you let them in too close, it's that you're still convinced that another person being disappointed in you takes away something essential from who you are.

It's not that you can't handle putting your creative work in public, it's that you still assume the possibility of criticism is a threat to your intrinsic value.

In all of our personal stories of this, it is never the thing, it always the thing after the thing that we fear. After the failure, after the criticism, after the humiliation, our greatest fear is that

somehow this means we are less valuable as a human being, because we believe these experiences subtract from who we are at our deepest level.

But they don't.

+ + +

In Mark 16, we see that Mary Magdalene, Mary the mother of Jesus, and Salome were the world's first preachers of the gospel, and the first ones to proclaim the resurrection.

Yes. Women were the first ones to proclaim the resurrection of Christ.

(And two thousand years later men are still arguing about whether or not women can preach the gospel, while they hold in their hand a Bible with a story about these three women proclaiming the resurrection and preaching the gospel.)

Churches. Men. Pastors.

Just stop it. (That's the extent of my engagement with that ridiculous way of thinking.)

Back to the story.

Three days before these women were first surprised by the resurrection, they saw Jesus get crucified. So when they came to the tomb, they did not see what they expected to see. They came expecting death, but they found life. They came expecting things to be the same, but they were different. They thought they were coming to ritualize the fact that it was over, but what they were met with was the unexpected vision that it had only just begun.

They found out that at the center of the life of Jesus and the cosmic story of our universe is the truth and power of resurrection.

The resurrection means the story of our world needs to be told differently.

Death became life.
Pain transformed to joy.
The end gave birth to a new beginning.

After my unexpected conversion experience at eighteen, I felt this deep sense of calling to become a pastor two years later. I did not know any pastors personally, I did not fully understand what it meant when I told people about it, but I did feel called.

At one point in graduate school, I was convinced I was going to get a Ph.D and stay in the academy and teach. Maybe what I assumed was a pastoral calling five years earlier could be lived out and expressed through my voice as a professor.

Of course, my potential Ph.D advisor left our seminary right before I started my last year, my work with him was stopped before it even started, and my future fell apart. With my new found openness to reimagining my future, I allowed myself to open up even more to helping lead a new church my friend Carl was going to start back in Honolulu.

After we met weekly for eight months to talk, to pray, and to dream about the future together with the church, he backed out of leading the church for family and medical reasons. When this happened, I still felt like the church was what God was inviting me into regardless of what happened with him.

When I explained that to him, he told me he already knew that, and that I just wasn't ready to hear that earlier—so he basically Jedi mind tricked me into becoming a church planter (even though I don't fully know what that means because I've never seen any Star Wars movies).

But as I look back, I know that my desire to be a professor was driven by both the love I have for teaching, and an unconscious desire to avoid ever having to face my greatest fears.

The two biggest fears I had in my twenties were failing publicly and disappointing people close to me.

What if I tell people about our desire and our plan to move back to Hawaii and start a church and it doesn't work?

What if I allow myself to truly care about something and have others be indifferent to it?

What if I finally create something that the past ten years of my life have prepared me to create and it doesn't work and everybody knows (by the way, its not everybody, we just think that)?

Up until the season we started Imagine, I wasn't ready to experience the potentially painful answers to those questions about failing.

Or, what if I let people into my life and offer to guide them, and they walk away?

What if I give my life to teaching and preaching, and the people around me come to the conclusion that I don't have what it takes?

What if the church fails, and all of our friends and family, mentors, and people who care about us and believe in us are disappointed in us?

Public failure. Personal disappointment. What would this say about me?

Even though Imagine was born and grew, and is still thriving seven years later, to some degree, every one of the fears I brought into this experience of starting and leading a church has come into being. I have disappointed people close to me. I have failed at certain elements of leading. I have seen many people I brought in close, cared about, and guided with all my heart walk away from the church and from me. There have been many instances where I have reflected on the state of the church and wondered if the people who knew us best would be disappointed by how we were doing.

And do you know what happened each time one of my greatest fears materialized?

Nothing.

I didn't disintegrate or spontaneously combust.

The universe did not suddenly implode.

Nothing happened.

Each time it was painful. And I sat with it, faced it, brought it in close, and shed some tears as I felt it and released it, and then nothing happened.

It wasn't the end, it was just painful. It didn't take anything away from me, it was just a temporary form of failure. It had no power to threaten any part of my inherent value in Christ, it was just a challenging relational loss.

To add to this, not only did failure not take away anything essential from me, it actually helped remove nonessential things off me.

The resurrection doesn't just mean the story of our world needs to be told differently, it means the story of your life needs to be told differently.

The resurrection means that the thing after the thing is nothing, or no thing at all. Humiliation means nothing. Failing means nothing. Criticism means nothing. Making a mistake means nothing.

And when I say nothing, what I mean is that whatever we assumed failure, loss, or embarrassment took away from who we are is a lie. That in and through each of those experiences, not only will nothing essential be taken away, but more of who you truly are will be revealed.

Hidden within the unacceptable forms of death are unimaginable gifts of life.

None of our greatest fears carry the power we believe they have to make judgments about who we are. Those three brave women who came to the tomb expecting death but ended up finding life show us that in all of the places of your life that you expect to find death, you can actually be met with life.

Resurrection life is not avoiding failure, it's the freedom that comes from accepting failure.

It is in no way escaping loss, it's the discovery of the love that is present in the loss.

Resurrection is not just God creating life out of death at that time with Jesus, resurrection is God creating life out of death at all times with you.

The resurrection means that the thing after the thing that we fear so deeply, is actually nothing at all.

NONDUAL AND NONCHALANT

Talking about non dual theory and consciousness is similar to talking about contemplation and zen. Which means most of the time, people are either completely disinterested, and thus not open, or assume they already know what you mean when you talk about it, so they are still not truly open.

But accepting this is part of waking up—when you're talking about depth and when you're sharing a vision of the further spiritual journey beyond inspiration and excitement, not everyone is going to tune in.

That's okay.

Also, there's something special about learning to trust and delight in what you see, even if others are not interested in learning about what you've seen. Rumi, when speaking of the power and poetry of his life with Spirit said, "You dance inside my chest where no one sees you."

I had this quote up on the wall in one of our apartments for a long time. I love it and resonate with it deeply because there is this beautiful and powerful experience you have when you're able to silently carry the vision and when you know that seeing and knowing for yourself is the true gift. (And by the way, I know I used this quote in the intro too.)

Now back to non dual theory.

How do speak of that which cannot be said? How do you conceptualize that which, by its very nature escapes conceptualization? How do you attempt to put into words the experience so others can know, even though it needs to be experienced to be known? How do you use the analytical tools of the mind to construct a mental image of something that transcends the very image you've created?

(I should have stopped here.)

First, nondual consciousness is not primarily a concept, it is a direct realization.

The nondual mind is able to embrace all of reality as a unified arising. This is why the brilliant Cynthia Bourgeault begins her book on centering prayer by saying that nondual consciousness is "the capacity to sense the whole pattern as a single unified field."

This simple, but endlessly profound phrase holds together the entire mystery, truth, and experience of the nondual. Before any labels, distinctions, judgments, differentiation, or analyzing of parts, the entire pattern of reality is taken in to the Self, and participated in as one thing.

Before it's many, it's one.

Before it's in parts, it's whole.

Before it's explained, it's embraced.

This mind is able to allow reality to be exactly what it is right now without needing to withdraw awareness from any part of it, without needing to exclude or change any part of it, and without needing to justify or fix any part of it.

It begins with pure acceptance.

You have to allow reality to hit you in all its truth, with all of its beauty, with all of its ugliness, and in all of its pain, and learn how to just let it be.

This is about letting go.

This radical letting go comes from a universal form of forgiveness that is extended not just to the individual pain you've experienced in your life, but to the cosmic imperfection that is present in life itself.

This universal allowing comes from the unimaginable releasing of every expectation on how life is supposed to be, in order to receive life for exactly what it is.

When our absolute attention to the dark is enveloped in an absolute awareness of the light, it becomes an unconditional acceptance of what is.

+ + +

Letting go of the need to change someone means you are finally free to love someone and let them be. And in the case of the nondual, this someone is not a someone, it is life itself.

The great Franciscan scientist and theologian Ilia Delio writes, "Heaven unfolds when we see things for what they are, not what we think they should be, and when we love others for who they are, and not what we expect them to be."

The boundaries between heaven and earth, good and bad, and light and darkness disappear in the center of your own heart as you accept and embrace the universe for exactly what it is. Here, we are simply mirroring back to creation what the creator is eternally doing for us.

I have always had these phrases or mantras that naturally emerge during my times in silence and contemplation. When these mantras arrive on my lips and are said out slowly and repeatedly, they communicate what I have directly realized, personally experienced, and have come to know for my self.

It's not just what I've learned, it's what I live.
It's not just what I believe, it's who I've become.
It's the moment where the Word has been made flesh.

One of the phrases I have said and experienced countless times during moments of silence, solitude, and prayer is "everything just is."

On my Grandpa's old roof in Los Angeles where I used to live, "everything just is."

On the 54th floor terrace of my old college in New York City, "everything just is."

On a boat during a surf trip in the middle of the Indian Ocean, "everything just is."

On a desert in Morocco sitting by myself, "everything just is."

On the edge of a mountain here in Hawaii, "everything just is."

And sitting in our old garage doing my morning silence in the middle of a huge mess, "everything just is."

Our old garage was a weird and open garage because it had three walls, and where the third wall was supposed to be, it was completely open and connected to the side of our house. Since, we used this garage as storage for our church the first four to five years, it was always filled with what I call sacred junk.

Sacred because of the memories and experiences they are attached to.

Junk because it just sits around after and takes up space.

While I would be sitting on this elevated part of the cement that framed the open space, meditating in silence, I would be surrounded by things like old rusty bikes with bent frames we didn't use anymore, or two cases of soda almost completely covered in weeds and plants that were left over from the first barbecue we had at our house. There was dirt that needed to be swept, random materials left over from events and exercises with Imagine, and plants around me that were withering and dying, mixed in and integrated with beautiful flowers that were blooming.

This small space was a microcosm for the whole of reality.

Life and death.
Beauty and ugliness.
Order and chaos.

This particular place is where I would move beyond the universal tension in life itself.

Richard Rohr says, "The struggle to forgive reality for being exactly what it is right now often breaks us through to non dual consciousness."

The allowing of grace in my imperfect garage became the acceptance of everything that is imperfect in the world.

Only the nondual mind can say with integrity that everything just is and truly mean it. The reality of death does not negate the power of life. Ugliness is able to comfortably co-exist in the same space as beauty without ever forcing you to choose a side. Chaos is embedded within the very order of life itself.

The nondual mind does not ignorantly compartmentalize imperfection or deny the darkness, it integrates imperfection and includes the darkness within a larger life space.

This is why the mystic can say, every thing is not good, but everything is okay.

This paradox short circuits the dualistic mind, breaks down our everyday categories of judgment, and enables us to break through to a higher level of seeing that can truly allow everything to just be.

For those who read about nondual theory or the nondual mind and think, what does any of this have to do with our day to day lived life?

First, great question. And here is the first thing.

You stop fighting reality.

We live on the thirty seventh floor in a forty three story condo tower in the urban core of

Honolulu, in a neighborhood called Kaka'ako.

No need to try and pronounce that.

What this means is our family spends a lot of time standing and dancing in elevators, and walking and running through hallways.

One of these days, while we were riding up on the elevator, my three year old daughter was

asking for something. After she asked, I told her that she may not have what she was asking for. And then in response, she hit me with the classic three year old question, which then was followed by one of my favorite exchanges we've had.

"Why?"

"Well, because now is not the time for that babe."

"Why?

"Because we don't always get what we want sweetie."

"Why?"

It kept going.

And what I love about these conversations is that if my daughter (or any kid) keeps asking the question why, eventually it forces us to zoom out and start giving answers in a more general and a more universal way about life.

And on this day after asking why multiple times, I finally and ultimately responded with,

"Because thats life baby!"

And as we walked down the hallway, my daughter resisted and responded by frustratingly repeating the phrase,

"This is not life! This is not life! This is not life!"

My neighbors were definitely worried for her.

See, in that moment, when my daughter exclaimed, "This is not life!" she was simply fighting reality (now, let's give her a developmental break, she was three when this happened).

While most people might find this story cute and silly, what we don't realize is that every instance we are frustrated with our circumstances, each time we are unwilling to accept a painful truth, and in all moments where it feels like we are grinding against life, we are all my three year old daughter defiantly exclaiming, "This is not life!"

Anger and frustration are always a form of nonacceptance.

The nondual mind does not fight reality because it accepts reality. It has the capacity to experience peace even when everything isn't peaceful. It does not get offended or disappointed at unmet expectations, because the nondual mind does not have expectations. It doesn't get surprised or shocked at suffering anymore because it has already embraced suffering as a a part of this unfinished world.

The nondual mind does not stay angry and it does not remain frustrated, because it always bends toward acceptance.

You will never hear the nondual mind shouting "This is not life" as it walks down the hallways of life.

+ + +

There is a difference between compulsion and compassion.

Now, with all of that said, in absolutely no way does the nondual mind mean that you stop caring for and being committed to work for healing and transformation in this world.

Being able to include the heart of the world does not mean you condone every part of the world. (And that rhymed, so you know it's true.)

The nondual space gives birth to a rugged commitment to humanity, to life long work for justice, for all kinds of culture shaping creativity, and to an unwillingness to settle for the status quo in our world—it is just the energy we carry as we do this work is transformed into something brand new.

You no longer work with compulsion, you work compassion.

Compulsion says "I need this to change or else I won't be at peace."

But compassion says "I want this to change and I will work to create change, but no matter what the outcomes are, it will not take my peace."

Compulsion still flows out of the ego's need to win, to prove, or to impress.

Compassion is liberated from that need to win, knows it has nothing to prove, and is simply here as a loving expression.

This is why Ken Wilber says,

> "Because of compassion, you will work your fingers to the bone, push the world until you literally bleed, toil till the tears stain your vision, struggle until life itself runs dry. And in the deepest, deepest center of your Heart, the World is already thanking you."

The compassion of the nondual mind allows you to be loyal to this world while remaining liberated from this world.

You no longer see the world as something to overcome.

What is so fascinating and telling in one of Jesus' last conversations with his disciples in John 16, is that he keeps on talking about joy. No matter how much people argue over their specific beliefs, regardless of the energy religious people spend wasting time on trying to decide who is in and who is out, Jesus keeps insisting this entire universe is built for joy.

Like Jesus, I still have the audacity to believe that this is all about joy.

And in this conversation, Jesus goes on to say, "I have told you these things, so that in me you may have peace. In this world you will have trouble. But take heart! I have overcome the world."

When the pain of reality was met by, embraced through, and overcome in Jesus, a path opened up for this same experience to become true in us.

This means that the pain of reality can also be met by, embraced through, and overcome in your very being. And when it's overcome in you, you will not longer resist it and wrestle against it in the world. You do not have to fight and overcome that which has already been overcome.

Shane Hipps, when referencing these words of Jesus, wrote, "Rather than changing its nature, Jesus offers us something better. He has overcome the world."

The acceptance, embrace, and overcoming of all of the pain, antagonisms, and suffering of the world, while sustaining an unguarded heart and an openness to Spirit, empowers us to break through to the nondual, and live with the absolute embrace of everything that is.

In other words, everything just is.

PEAKS AND PATHS

There's a story about a kid who said that while he was on LSD, he discovered the meaning of life. So, the next morning, he woke up and shared this exciting and groundbreaking revelation with his friends. So, naturally they responded by eagerly asking him what was the real meaning of life.

The kid thought for a second and said, "I forgot."

Now, the extremes of this story—the discovery of the meaning of life followed by the forgetting of what it was—are what make the story funny and ridiculous. But, packed into this compact little exchange between friends is a powerful message about the nature of the spiritual quest.

The story expresses how a spiritual experience doesn't always translate into a spiritual life.

We can have a powerful experience of God and walk away without being transformed in a permanent way. We can be convinced that we have truly overcome something deep within, only to fall back into the same pattern within a week of the experience.

Or, like in the kid's case in the story, we can discover the meaning of life and then forget what it was the next morning.

This can be frustrating, discouraging, and can leave us feeling kind of helpless in our pursuit of growth and change.

We've gotten a glimpse, but can not seem to move closer to the goal. We have seen something true revealed, but we don't know how to translate the revealing into a lived reality. We have traveled to the top of the mountain and reached the peak that enabled us to see, but the peak was never meant to be the place we were supposed to stay.

This particular experience shows up in many different forms.

You went to some big Christian conference, heard all the inspiring speakers, took rigorous notes on all the topics, and during that time of worship you stretched your hands as high as you could. And with tears streaming down your face, you knew God was with you, you knew you could overcome the past, and you believed things would be completely different in the future.

But by the next Friday, things were the same.

Or, you went on your pilgrimage to Burning Man, went to Joshua tree and ate some mushrooms with friends, you paid for a three day workshop on overcoming your ego—and through experiences like this, you believed you were born again. And after this experience, you were completely inspired to live differently as a result.

But by the next Friday, things were the same.

So, what do we usually do?

We go back.

We go back to try and re-create the environment, believing another intense experience is going to be the key for our transformation and a more liberated future.

We go to another Christian conference. We go to another deliverance night. We do the next twenty-one day fast. We raise our hands even higher, we shed tears with even more desperation, hoping and praying that somehow this next peak experience of God is going to be the final piece that makes the puzzle of our life fit together.

This can become a cycle.

Or we go back to Burning Man, we go on another psychedelic trip, we visit a different psychic, we start doing sound baths instead of sensory deprivation tanks, secretly trying to make the perfect spiritual cocktail that is going to bring the stability and peace we need for our life.

This also can become a cycle.

There's a story about a little girl who was scared of the dark because she believed there was a monster who would appear in the corner of the room whenever the lights would go out. She would lay in her bed in with a silent anxiety and paralyzing fear until she would finally scream for her dad to come into the room. And each time the dad would come in, he would flip on the lights, she would see that there was no monster in her room, and then as her dad sat next to her, she would slowly go back to sleep.

She would do this night after night after night.

Of course there is a great sense of comfort and an immediate relief of fear whenever the dad comes in and turns the light on. Each time, the young girl is temporarily convinced that there is no monster, which then alleviates her fear and eventually enables her to go back to sleep the rest of the night. While the momentary peace is great, the real issue for the girl becoming free from fear and anxiety is not how quickly her dad can run in to turn on the light, it's her learning to trust that she's safe even while she's in the dark.

What she sees in the light needs to become what she trusts in the dark. The truth of what she saw needs to be transformed into the truth of what she lives, which is her knowing there is no monster. This dynamic speaks to the heart of the relationship between peak spiritual experiences, and learning to live a spiritual life.

The peak needs to become a path.
The vision needs to be transformed into values.
The spiritual high needs to turn into solid ground.

Each time we go back to re-create the powerful experience we had, manufacture another massive God experience in order to feel something, or call dad in to flip the light switch back on, we are going backwards.

The spectacular event is a glimpse, not the goal.

It's the revealing, not the full reality.

It's the peak that enables us to see, it's not the place that we are supposed to stay.

Cynthia Bourgeault says that faith is "Not just admiring Jesus, but acquiring his consciousness."

Here, is where we have the best chance to see how central contemplation is for a life that can transition between believing in Jesus to becoming in Christ.

Contemplation is where ecstasy becomes identity.

It is in the wide open, spacious, attentive, and unhurried presence of contemplation where we can move from believing to becoming, from learning to living, and from experiencing to embodying.

In this translucent space of silence, we directly realize we do not need to flip the light switch on again to see what we've already seen, but rather, we need to sit in this space of the subtle light of the Spirit and learn to trust the new world the light has already shown.

In the quiet sanctuary of our own presence, we know we do not need to return to the mountain top to listen to the voice of God booming again from the heavens, we need to remember what God has already spoken and practice hearing the truth of these words from our own heart.

In the unhurried movement of being still, we do not need to synthetically manufacture another explosive God experience to feel God's presence, what we need is to stay still long enough so that even the most subtle touch of the Spirit becomes a felt invitation into the further unfolding of our life.

Without contemplation, even our most powerful experiences of God will not turn into a peaceful life in God.

+ + +

At eighteen, and within a couple months after my spontaneous awakening moment with the Spirit, I drove up to a wealthy gated community twenty-five minutes outside of Los Angeles where I used to go to parties, to spend time in silence.

I memorized the code to get into this beautiful gated community the one time I went there to party.

Just in case.

(Although when I memorized the code, I'm pretty sure the just in case did not include me needing a quiet space to talk to God.)

But as I drove through these amazing houses, I found an empty lot with a beautiful bluff, and a single chair at the edge, overlooking this vast space toward Downtown LA. It felt as if it was a personal pew created for me in this great cosmic cathedral.

And as I sat down on that chair by myself, for the first time in my life, without the aid of mushrooms, the unified field of reality opened up for me. My monkey mind was silenced, and I was fully present to myself, to God, and to life. It was where Thich Nhat Hanh's words became flesh for me for the first time when he said, "The miracle is not to walk on water. The miracle is to walk on the green earth in the present moment."

For the first time I could feel a singular flow of my own consciousness, the presence of God, and the whole of reality seamlessly flow in me, around me, and as me. It was light, it was peace, and it was love. It was all of life gracefully held together in, wonderfully animated by, and emanating forth from the universal flow of Christ.

I even distinctively remember watching and listening to the rapidly fluttering wings of two hummingbirds moving in unison near me, and saying out loud to myself, "Oh there you are God."

I know.

Very weird.

I mean, I was still smoking weed at the time.

But, here's why this story is important.

What I could only see before when I was standing at the peak of my highest high, I was starting to see as I was sitting on the plateau of my daily life.

Spectacular spiritual experiences are like a gate we go through in order to be in awe, to feel at peace, and to temporarily touch that which is most true about our universe.

What do the mystics always say about what is true?

We are loved.
We are safe.
We are seen.
We are enough.
Life is a miracle.
Everything is connected.

Existence is amazing.
Spirit is in everything.
We're going to be okay.

If peak spiritual experiences are the gate we go through to access the truth, contemplation is the discovery that there is no gate.

In contemplation, we realize for ourselves that the God we experienced up there is present and available right here.

Contemplation slowly grounds the wisdom we've received into the depths of our being, plants it firmly in our hearts, and unites it with our bodies. It solidifies what we have seen with our eyes and catalyzes it into what we know in our Spirit. It is where we go from translating the world differently due to new insights, to transforming the very "I" that is seeing through these new translations.

Contemplation transforms what we saw at the peak into who we are on the path.

Which leaves us with these questions.

Why would I climb back up to the mountain top to see the view of the terrain I am already living in?

Why would I pay money to people to let me in a gate that provides me with temporary access to that which requires no gate?

Why would I need to turn the lights on again when I am already living with the vision that came to me from turning them on?

Why would I fly to another country to visit an ashram to experience the depth of the God who is already fully present in the sanctuary of my own presence?

Once you are on the new path that you saw from the peak, you no longer need to go back to the peak itself. That would be going backwards.

SOCIAL LADDERS, VICARIOUS VALUE, AND CAREER CHOICES

Freedom has always been one of the most important words for my life, and one of the central pursuits of my life.

The most powerful dimension of freedom I dreamt of and longed for in my own life was personal and spiritual (being a cis gender, straight, middle class, white male in the United States of America, I lived with the kind of privilege as a kid that did not require me to think about economic and political freedom in the way BIPOC have been forced to).

As a seventeen and eighteen year old in the middle of a deep existential crisis and ground shaking spiritual opening into what felt like nothingness, I could feel the power of meaninglessness lurking, but I could also sense the real possibilities of freedom calling.

Freedom meant I could just be, and be okay.

Freedom meant I would feel the exact same about who I was regardless of whether people applauded me or not.

Freedom meant that the peace I carried would not be contingent upon any external form.

Or, at least at seventeen, that was how I saw it.

I was successful, I got attention, and I was treated as one of the special people because of things I could do in sports and music, but I had also realized something—I was not free.

With all of that said, freedom meant more than just the personal sense. I wanted to be freed from an entire culture that sees people's value based on what they can do for them socially, where they can get them professionally, and a culture that almost demands people who want to be successful to sometimes treat other people as a means to an end. I grew up using people, manipulating people, climbing the social ladder, and buying into the unspoken rule of the system—get attention and achieve status by any means necessary.

I didn't just want to be free spiritually by knowing who I was, I wanted to be free socially so I could see others for who they were.

Or, at least at eighteen, that was how I saw it.

+ + +

In 2012, right before I moved back to Hawaii to take our first daring step to start our church, I spent the last four months in Orange County, California, shadowing a few of my friends and peers that were pastors. I figured since I was never on staff at a church before, I should probably get a little bit of experience before I started a church.

Not enough to normalize elements of the church culture and system I wanted nothing to do with, but enough to know what a meeting was actually like.

One of the guys who I shadowed and spent some time with was my friend Dwight.

Dwight was a little bit older than me, a part of a close learning community of mine in grad school focused on studying Black Theology, and he was also a pastor of a beautiful, vibrant, and predominantly black church in Los Angeles. During this season of shadowing, we had made plans for me to come and be with his church on a Sunday, sit in on some meetings after, and get a feel for what a day in his life on a Sunday looked like. I was excited to be around a leader who I respected, and grateful to see some of the inner happenings of his church.

Two days before that particular Sunday, another friend of mine told me he was going to be in San Diego all day shooting a video with one of the biggest names in the Christian publishing

industry. This person not only had a colossal following, they were also a personal hero of mine. So when this invitation was extended to me, I could immediately sense my ego start to justify why it would be okay to cancel on my friend Dwight, and go to San Diego for this opportunity.

"Its not like I can't visit Dwight's church on another day."

"Dwight wouldn't mind, he's a friend, it's no big deal." (Even though if I did cancel, I probably wouldn't tell him the exact reason.)

"This could be a once in a lifetime opportunity to meet this person and hang out with them."

But despite the volume of that voice in that internal dialogue, I decided to stick to my original plans, spend the day with Dwight and his community, and deny the invitation to hang out with one of my writing heroes.

My ego knew that spending time with this author was a better strategy for climbing the social ladder to the top of the Christian industrial complex, but my true self knew that this ladder was just the Christian version of the same thing I wanted to be liberated from needing to climb since I was seventeen.

While referring to the way Jesus related to those around him, Cynthia Bourgeault said, "He embraced everyone and everything but took nothing to Himself for his own profit. People were not manipulated; they did not become fodder for his spiritual ambitions or his animal instincts."

It seems that in order to follow the Jesus who refused to use or manipulate others for his own agenda, we must also refuse to use or manipulate people for ours.

My ego knew that spending the day in San Diego would be better for a career as one of those special Christian figures who writes books and speaks on stages

(feel free to throw up after you read that),

but my true self knew spending the day in Los Angeles with my gracious guide of a friend was another step forward in integrity and alignment with the actual way of Jesus

(which, let's be honest, is not the kind of thing the Christian industrial complex is most concerned about).

My ego knew that developing a relationship with someone who is an already established public figure with status is good for "business," but my true self knew that nothing is more powerful and valuable than having an actual friend who knows you, sees you, and cares about you.

My ego was willing to sacrifice an actual gesture of love and relationship from a friend for a chance to be near people who the culture (one that I wanted nothing to do with) deems as important or as having a certain status, but my true self knew that to do that would be to perpetuate insecure elements of Christian culture I believe we are supposed to be transcending.

Here, I saw that the same ladders that were available for me to climb as a seventeen year old fighting to elevate my status in the streets or with music, were still here in front of me as a twenty eight year old getting ready to begin the adventure of starting a new church.

The only difference was now they just happened to be propped up against massive building that said "Jesus" on the front.

+ + +

Vicarious value has its own economy.

Vicarious value is one of the most powerful invisible forces in our influencer culture in general, and in the Christian industrial complex specifically.

Vicarious value is one of the most socially acceptable forms of status seeking, and one of the silliest dynamics in popular church culture today.

So, what is vicarious value?

Vicarious value is the belief that when we are connected with someone of perceived social status and value, it increases our value.

When speaking of the power of social value and celebrity, Gary Laderman, in his book, "Sacred Matters" argues that "It is a power that is not shared equally among all societal members, and those that do not have it will search for ways to get access to it."

This is why we care about social status.

This is why name dropping is a thing.

And this is why getting tagged in photos with people who have a bigger following than you on Instagram means something to us.

This is why we quietly bend conversations in order to insert moments we shared or conversations we had with people who occupy a higher social status than us. Vicarious value means that we believe and live as if the status and value of someone else is able to transfer onto us if we are close to or connected with them.

Nobody talks about it. Everybody does it.

(Not everybody.)

Despite the fact that Jesus' brother writes in the book of James, "My brothers and sisters, believers in our glorious Lord Jesus Christ must not show favoritism…" then proceeds to go on to describe the evil of showing special treatment and attention to the rich, well dressed, and those with higher social status. He even finishes by saying, "But if you show favoritism, you sin and are convicted by the law as lawbreakers."

I see a lot of climbing of social ladders in the Christian Industrial Complex, and almost comical exchanges of vicarious value taking place with Christian celebrities and the actual celebrities they want to be like.

Years ago, I remember seeing a high profile pastor saying that he was going to spend the week highlighting people on his Instagram who are special, and have come to or are a part of his church. And then I see him posting pictures of actors, television personalities, and famous musicians who he has relationships with or took pictures with at his church.

I just remember thinking, "That's so weird."

What is the driving force for a pastor to intentionally draw attention to the fact that you personally know famous people, or that celebrities attend your church? The answer is obvious to everyone who is not caught up in it.

There is an invisible economy of vicarious value that pop Christianity is held captive by.

When a pastor consistently name drops celebrities in their teachings or public appearances, what I see at work is the invisible economy of vicarious value.

When I see pastors intentionally (and quite obviously) drawing attention to and highlighting their connections and relationships with celebrities through social media, what I see at work is the invisible economy of vicarious value.

When I see Christian leaders putting a spotlight on the presence of celebrities in their worship gatherings or circuses (I meant conferences), what I see at work is the invisible economy of vicarious value.

Now, the people who are trading in and capitalizing on this economy of vicarious value do so not just for personal gain and brand elevation, they do so for the advancement of their churches or creative endeavors as well. And in their defense, the majority of relational transactions that take place within this economy happen at an unconscious level, which means the core intentions of these behaviors are not always recognizable to the person making them.

Because as we know, it's all for the glory of God right?

Wink wink.

Which is why if you were to ask pastors and leaders why they bring into the public light the nature of their relationships with celebrities, you would more than likely hear some answer about how it brings attention to and focus on Jesus. While clearly being able to leverage the

relationships for their own agenda and advancement, the entire relationship would exist under the banner of glorifying God or the ironic statement of wanting to make Jesus famous.

The theologian Roger Olson writes, "Americans are obsessed with celebrities. Evangelical Americans are obsessed celebrities who convert to evangelical Christianity by being born again."

I would argue that this statement by Olson only makes sense because of this invisible economy of vicarious value. The internal logic of vicarious value says when we are connected with someone of perceived social status and value, it increases our value. But, the fascinating dynamic is that this perceived value does not only transfer to an individual (through their personal connection), it also can transfer to a church (through their institutional connection).

"Chris Pratt is so cool (which means he has more social value) and he's a Christian!"

"And guess what? Sometimes he comes to our church! Doesn't that make our church cool (or have more value)?"

"Yeah!"

If this celebrity who has a high social status and perceived value talks about me or our church, it brings more credibility and value to all of the connected parties. If it was not believed that the establishing of a connection between a celebrity and a pastor or a church brought some form of value, it would never be highlighted.

To those with eyes to see this invisible economy, its not hard to spot and its always ridiculous to see.

+ + +

Since I started pastoring Imagine in the Summer of 2013, I've been to one big Christian conference. I was asked to come and be a part of a panel discussion. And in the midst of the lights, the music, the fog machines, the Jesus junk, the guest speakers, the green rooms, and the palpable neurotic energy, what I remember the most is one conversation I had backstage with one of the speakers.

She was high energy, she was happy to be there, she was hilarious, and she definitely seemed like she knew the drill when it came to these conferences. She was also an already established writer and speaker, who since then has blown up and expanded her brand and reach exponentially.

While we were backstage talking, I started sharing about the heart of our church Imagine, how these conferences weren't really my vibe, the authenticity that was central to my life as a pastor, I could tell she was genuinely drawn in and interested in what I was saying.

Even though there was much more to the exchange, I do vividly remember her telling me how deep down she wanted to be able to do some of the things I was doing or say some of the things I was saying,but how she couldn't, because if she did, she would lose her audience.

And based on where her career has gone since then, she has definitely not lost her audience, and in fact, has grown that audience into a massive following.

She may not have realized it at the time, but she was pretty clear that her audience was a higher priority than her integrity.

I wasn't surprised.

I wasn't let down.

I wasn't angry.

What I felt was more of this deep internal sigh that silently communicated, "Oh yeah, thats what we're doing here huh?"

It wasn't truth, integrity, and authenticity, it was success, career outcomes, and building an audience.

And of course, it would be all done in the name of Jesus.

The one who paid no attention to the status quo.

The one who lived with infinite integrity.

The one who embodied such counter cultural authenticity, that he not only lost an audience, but actually got killed.

It would be done in the name of that Jesus.

It was in the name of the One who always chose authenticity over an audience that this Christian cultural figure told me she was unwilling to lose her audience as a result of her authenticity.

This is what I call a tragic and comedic form of irony.

Social ladders, vicarious value, and these career choices are three of the main pillars that hold up the kind of culture that exists in the Christian Industrial complex that, at eighteen, I already saw through and longed to be liberated from.

I thought freedom meant we were supposed to move beyond having eyes that focus on who in the room has the potential to elevate our status, and being able to control the body that is being drawn to them as a result. I assumed everyone—especially the most public followers of Jesus—saw that the dehumanizing mode of treating others as a means to an end was one of the first things that we're supposed to say no to when we decide to yes to Jesus. I imagined a future where following Jesus meant we already have received the conclusion from God about who we are, and thus, would be able to see through the invisible economy of vicarious value.

Sometimes while we're climbing the ladder to the top we are unable to hear the words of Jesus who has his feet firmly planted on the ground.

SOUR PUNCH AND ILLUSIONS

One of the first deep moments of reflection I can remember was when I was about ten years old. It involved my living room, my kitchen, a bag of sour punch straws, and some unexpected reflections on desire and satisfaction.

I found myself caught up in a cycle of eating candy, wanting more candy, wondering why I kept eating more candy, and ultimately realizing that more candy wasn't actually going to satisfy me.

I know.

Very weird.

I was sitting in my living room watching TV, when I remembered there was an entire bag of sour punch straws in the kitchen. So I got up, walked into the kitchen, tore open the bag, grabbed a handful, and went back to the couch and ate them all.

Then I realized something.

I wanted more.

So, I got up, walked back to the kitchen, poured myself another handful, and sat back down on the couch, and ate every last one. As soon as I finished that second round of sour punch straws, you can imagine what my next thought was. I wanted more. So, I got up again, and repeated the predictable cycle I was in.

What changed the third or fourth time was that when I walked into the kitchen to get a hold of another handful, I told myself while I was on the way, "This is the last one."

But as soon as I sat down on the couch again and swallowed those last little bits of soury (is soury a word?) sugar chunks down my throat, I instantaneously knew that what I told myself before was a lie. So I got up again, convincing myself on the way that this, in fact, would truly be my last trip to the kitchen, only to discover that once again, that statement to myself was a lie.

At about the fifth or sixth trip to the kitchen, my internal dialogue shifted dramatically. While my ten year old body was moving toward the kitchen as if there was a magnetic pull in place I did not have the power to resist, I no longer told myself that this was going to be the last trip.

But I did start to ask myself some pretty serious questions.

Why am I eating more? Is this actually making me satisfied? Why can't I stop eating? Am I even enjoying this? Why would I think the next handful is going to satisfy me when the first five or six handfuls didn't do it?

So obviously, I grabbed the rest, sat down on the couch, ate them all, and kept watching TV.

But as I sat there with those sugary fingers and an unsettled stomach, the unsettledness in me was deeper than the expected ache that comes from eating way too much candy. This unanticipated discomfort was connected to those questions I kept asking myself about desires, the attempt to fulfill desires, and the lack of satisfaction I was left with when I did fulfill them.

This was the first time I began wrestling with the reality of illusions.

Put simply, an illusion is simply a false idea or belief we have about how life works.

But when it comes to the spiritual life, illusions usually refer to false beliefs we have about that which is ultimate:

what is going to bring us joy,
what is going set us free,
and where we are going to find peace, contentment, and life.

So when we talk about illusions, we are speaking of the spaces and places we look too for our ultimate desires, and how they always end up disappointing us and not delivering on what they promise.

So what would be some of the most obvious examples of illusions in our culture today?

Becoming famous is what will make me feel loved and valued.

Getting married will complete me.

Attaining financial security will give me peace.

Having complete control over my life will make feel secure.

(How many of those boxes did you tick?)

The power of illusions manifests itself through the demands they make on our time, the energy they take from us while we try and obtain them, and through the grief we feel when they are finally exposed for the truth of what they are.

When it comes to illusions, the things that are always on the way are actually getting in the way.

This is why transcending our illusions is always about refusing to spend time on things that don't matter. It's about not expecting things to give something to us that they don't have the power to give, and it's about not looking for things to give us the life God is already and always offering us freely.

+ + +

The first step toward transcending and letting go of our illusions is the recognition of the shape of these illusions.

When you zoom out, gain some altitude, and see some of what drives humanity beneath the surface, there are only a few major illusions that exist in the world. Some of these consistent bigger picture illusions are:

Power, prestige, and possessions. (Thank you Richard Rohr.)

Safety and security, power and control, and affection and esteem. (Thank you Thomas Keating.)

Attention, affluence, and affection. (I think I came up with this one.)

One of the main reasons it can be so challenging to recognize the illusions in your life is because they keep trying to convince you that the real problem is that you need more of them.

This is why every time you obtain your desire and it does not satisfy you, the object of your desire explains to you how the real issue is that you don't have enough.

Whether it's attention, power, material goods, forms of financial security, sexual experiences, or using drugs, each time you seek out and fulfill your desire, it leaves you wanting more and believing that the next attempt at getting it is the one that will finally make you content. We're always so close to finally receiving the contentment we want, but never quite there.

Maybe the problem is not that we don't have enough of a particular thing, it's simply the thing itself.

Liberation from illusions comes when we realize it is not that we need more of the thing we are using, but rather that the very nature of the thing we are using does not have the power to give us what we want.

Here are a couple examples of how illusions work on scales.

If I'm the best baseball player, people will see me and I will feel whole.

I'm the best tee ball player ⟶ I'm the best in my little league ⟶ I'm the best baseball player in the state ⟶ I'm one of the top ranked baseball players in college ⟶ I'm a professional baseball player. (Am I whole now?)

Financial Security is the only thing that will give me peace and security.

If I get into this great college and study finance ⟶ If my internship turns into this great first job ⟶ If I finally make $100K a year ⟶ If I can buy a home and start building a solid 401k ⟶ If I can create a completely sold financial safety net for my future. (Am I now completely at peace?)

Hidden within so many of our pursuits is an illusion that is driving us with out us even knowing it.

Being the best at every level, achieving each goal, or reaching your desired social status will give you the same things—attention, admiration, recognition—it's just that at each stage as you get more and more of each of the same thing, it never fundamentally changes the experience it produces in you.

This is of course, why Thomas Merton says, "People may spend their whole lives climbing the ladder of success only to find, once they reach the top, that the ladder is leaning against the wrong wall."

You dream, sacrifice, work hard, and finally get to the top of the ladder, only to experience that it did not just magically click, it did not make you immediately whole, and the platform you now stand on does not change you in the depths of your life.

This is where illusions always lead us.

+ + +

In 2011, Aaron Rodgers won The Super bowl as the starting quarterback for the Green Bay packers, and was named Super Bowl MVP.

There is no higher peak in professional football on the entire planet, no greater achievement you can attain, and no greater accomplishment than what Aaron Rodgers earned on that day.

This is a guy who felt overlooked and under appreciated his whole football career. Coming out of High School, he did not get recruited by any major division one schools, and went to a junior college for two years before transferring to Cal. He did not have a conventional path toward becoming one of the best quarterbacks of all time, which would make reaching the Zenith of the football universe on that Super Bowl Sunday even more of an amazing and satisfying experience.

And as Rodgers stood on the podium that Super Bowl Sunday holding the championship and MVP trophies, he says,

> "I had that realization when I was at the top of my game, on the podium, winning the Super Bowl, and I kinda just looked around going, 'God, I love football so much, but there's gotta be something else.' And I repeated that and I didn't feel any reservation about it."

One of the most visible and successful professional athletes in the world, standing on the highest podium you can be on, and he looks out and keeps saying,

"There's gotta be something else."

"There's gotta be something else."

"There's gotta be something else."

It is only when you feel the powerlessness of an illusion for yourself that you will begin to be released from the power it has over you. We all have to open up that beautifully wrapped present that carries our illusion and see for ourselves that there is nothing inside.

Which is why illusions are connected to us being free.

Real freedom is not about telling someone to stop doing something because it's bad, it's about inviting them to let go of it because it's not working.

In 1 Corinthians 10, Paul wrote to the people in Corinth and said, "Everything is permitted, but everything isn't beneficial. Everything is permitted, but everything doesn't build others up."

Here's the thing about Corinth, this city had a larger than life reputation for trouble. There was a cultural phrase that was used during the first century, "to become Corinthianized." Which meant to be corrupted by the shameless, perverse, and greedy identity of the city through exposure. Even as Paul wrote to the church, there were people in the Corinthian church heavily involved with prostitution, a young man having sex with his step mom, and status and power issues. It was as dysfunctional as a community as it could be.

(Which is why when I preach about this church at Imagine, I always say, "No matter how many mistakes we all make, no matter how much we feel like we keep messing up our life, at least no one here is having sex with their step parent. See! We're doing better than the early church!")

So Paul is writing to people who live with no filter when it comes to satiating their cravings and have no limitations when to comes to fulfilling any desire they have.

And how does Paul engage this unique community that exists within this broader culture?

He doesn't shame them, he doesn't try to control their behavior, he doesn't use anger or any manipulative tactics. He simply names the truth that they have the freedom to do whatever they want, but also tries to show them that everything they want doesn't actually deliver the good that they are seeking.

So when Paul says, "Everything is permitted, but everything isn't beneficial…" he is essentially saying that while you have the freedom to do any thing you want, what I am revealing is that just because you can do it, does not mean, in the end it is going to bring you more joy, make you free, or deliver to you what you are asking it to give you.

Paul's talking about their illusions.

Paul names the things that are driving them and essentially says,

"Yes, you have the right to do that. You have the right to spend all of your energy on fulfilling that desire, you have the right to do whatever you want, no one is trying to control that, no one is trying to stop you from doing that. But here's what I am asking, "Is that thing you are pursuing actually leading you to the life it promises? Is that thing delivering what you believe it is supposed to deliver?"

This is why there a few questions I ask people who are wrestling with their illusions and not yet in a place where they are are ready to let go of them:

How many times do you have to taste something to know it isn't good?

How many times do you have to experience something to know it isn't real?

How many times do you have to try something to know it isn't working?

I can always tell pretty quickly if people are genuinely interested in seeing through their illusions in order to move beyond them, or if they're still just playing with them and complaining about them with no real intention of letting them go.

True freedom does not come from resisting a behavior because it is not right, it comes from realizing for yourself that the illusion is not real. You can resist something, but at a deeper level, still believe in the illusion within it.

+ + +

Letting go of illusions creates space for newness.

The brilliant Vietnamese monk Thich Nhat Hanh said, "For things to reveal themselves to us, we need to be ready to abandon our views about them."

When the hollowness, the emptiness, and the impotence of an illusion is revealed to us and experienced by us, the organic movement forward will be to let go of it.

You don't hold on to things you don't believe in.

And you can only be pulled in by things that you do.

So when we abandon our views on these illusions, a vast space of potential will open up within us, and a new horizon of possibility will emerge in our life. We will see new ways to give ourselves to the world that are actually meaningful, freed from the need for ego validation, and exciting to our true self with a fresh energy.

But simultaneously, we might be faced with fear, worry, and a sense of resistance, because the illusion doesn't only open us up to taking ahold of the new, it demands the courage to let go of the old.

So, when Merton says, "People may spend their whole lives climbing the ladder of success only to find, once they reach the top, that the ladder is leaning against the wrong wall." This raises the question about what we are supposed to do when we come to this realization and our illusions are exposed?

Should we, out of fear, stay on the ladder and keep climbing and deny the truth of what we have seen?

Or do we jump off, trusting that anytime we make a decision out of truth, integrity, and authenticity, somehow things are going to be okay (think that might be called faith)?

People are terrified of letting go of their illusions because they can see what it is going to cost them, and they are not ready to accept the consequences. This is one of the greatest inhibitors toward people relinquishing their illusions, and thus one of the greatest inhibitors for our life.

Accepting that illusion means you might leave that job, which means you won't make all that money, which is going to change your lifestyle.

Accepting that illusion means you don't care about climbing that ladder of success anymore, which means you won't be leveraging everything you have to get more noticed, which ultimately means you may never be as publicly recognized as you always wanted.

Accepting that illusion means you will walk away from that whole career, which means you are going to have to start over, which requires you to take a massive leap into uncertainty.

The moment the illusion begins to be revealed, something within us wants to fight it.

We've worked so hard to get to where we are, we've sacrificed so much to climb higher, we know what it will cost us if we walk away, and we are terrified of what will happen to us if we end up in that place of unknown when the illusion and its lifestyle pass by.

And yet, that space we are the most terrified of and spend so much energy trying to avoid is the very space where our life will begin again.

More alive.
More aligned.
More authentic.

More in tune with the frequency of the Spirit at home in the flow of God.

This is where we discover that the only things we ever let go of are the things that were getting in the way in the first place.

That lifestyle change is not worth more than your integrity. Not being publicly recognized does not take away from who you are, and even more so, it creates the possibility to experience the power of being seen and recognized by the gaze of God, which will give you the very thing you were looking for in the first place.

That space of starting over that your ego relates to as the end is nothing but the sacred site of you being born again.

In other words, put the sour punch straws down. You know they're not working. And they're probably going to make you sick.

SOMETHING TO RUN FOR

One of the initiatives we started through Imagine that I am most proud of is called Saying Grace.

Saying Grace is a four week journey of curated gatherings of dinners and stories between the church and the LGBTQ community. It is an experience with half straight people and half LGBTQ people that creates space for people to encounter each other as humans, connect with each other's hearts, and begin to have hopeful conversations and real relationships that will lead us to a shared future.

This group is led by Dr. Jade Higa—a teacher and former professor at University of Hawaii, who is both Queer and Christian, and myself. It has become this powerful space where the people we talk about become the people we talk to, where the stories we misunderstand from a distance

become the stories we begin to understand at our dinner tables, a place where hostility is transformed into Christ-shaped hospitality.

This four week experience is held together by mutual vulnerability, the church learning to listen, having hard and honest conversations within the envelope of connection and relationship, and ending in a living room with a powerful moment of prayer and song.

Saying Grace is one of those holy and heavy spaces where it feels like you are in the center of God's heart hearing it beat, and feeling the palpitation with every word spoken and every story shared.

Here…

I have seen a conservative middle aged woman, with a conventional faith, strumming a guitar in worship, while a young bisexual man prays for her with with a groundedness in the Spirit she may have never imagined was possible or acceptable.

I have seen young women tell their story of growing up and learning about and understanding their same sex attraction for the first time, and share how healing it was to do so in the presence of the church.

I have seen multiple people actually come out for the first time publicly during Saying Grace because they saw, experienced, and received this invitation from the church as an even bigger invitation from God to be honest about who they were.

Between the gut wrenching stories of being rejected by family because of their sexual identity, to the connection made though the shared tears around the table, and the new community that was forged through the Spirit over good food and wine, Saying Grace has become a defining thing for our church and for all of the individuals who have experienced it.

+ + +

A couple years ago, after making a short film about Saying Grace, we decided to have a film night on this beautiful deck in the heart of Chinatown here in Honolulu. Like any other day of an event, preparing and setting everything up was crazy.

You're dealing with food, drinks, design, audio, visual, moving furniture around, running to get things last minute, and on top of all of that, it was one of the most humid days I have ever felt here in Hawaii. There was absolutely no wind, it looked like it might rain on us, and the heat and humidity it created made it feel like we were all speed walking through a steam room for a couple hours.

It was sticky.

Right near the end of the setting up when people were close to arriving, we realized we had issues with audio and connectivity. The entire night was centered around the showing of this film, and what we call a "talk story" immediately after. Without audio, it doesn't work.

After some guidance from the audio guy for what we needed, I ran (and I mean ran) to a Walmart a block and half around the corner, jogged through the Walmart, ran up the escalator, picked out the cord I thought we needed through my blurred vision from the anxiety and adrenaline, payed for it, jogged back through the Walmart, ran through Chinatown back to the venue to give the audio guy the cord.

He told me it was the wrong one.

I screamed a little on the inside, sighed, and turn around and started running again.

I did the exact same thing, came back, and he told me the cord was the right one, but we needed an adaptor.

Knowing I did not have the time to cry or the desire to scream in public, I went through the exact same maddening process again!

I ran through China town, in and through Walmart, and bought another cord. All of the while, due to the impossibly wet humidity, along with my unexpected cardio blast, I was dripping sweat. It was the kind of sweat, where unless you're working out, it makes you look insane to be out in public.

So, I purchased the cord, ran back down the escalator, jogged though Walmart, and got outside. This time as I was running through the crowds, climbing up stairs, and jumping off curbs into the middle of busy streets, I had this massive smile on my face and I was laughing to my self.

It was one of those moments where you are outside of yourself watching yourself, knowing how crazy you look, but you cannot stop laughing because you are having the best time.

So, I made it back to the venue, gave the guy the cord, went to my car and blasted the air conditioner as I wet wiped myself down while I was changing for the event. By the serendipity of the Spirit, I made it back to the event for opening drinks, the showing of the film, and the amazing conversation after.

And that night as I looked back on that adrenaline drenched scene of me running through the streets of China Town with a huge smile on my face, all I could think was that

I was so happy I had something in my life I was willing to run for.

SECOND HALF OF LIFE

There is the first half of life and there is the second half of life.

Like The Buddha saying, "Enlightenment is not a matter of age…" these two unique stages of life are not defined by duration of time or how old we are, they are marked by degrees of growth, personal evolution, and when the ego is no longer in the driver's seat of the journey.

We need more pioneers into the second half of life, so we can have more guides through the second half of life.

To provide language for the transition between the first and second half of life not only helps people see the wider and more grounded pilgrimage ahead, it provides solidarity for those who have already intuited and started walking into this future. Giving people the language for this transitional shift is one of the most important gifts one can give, because this is one of the most critical steps some will take.

We live in a culture where people keep getting older without becoming real elders.

A few questions.

What is the second half of life? How does the second half of life feel different than the first? How does the nature of seeing itself change from the first to the second half of life?

In the second half of life:

You move from being driven by your ego to being drawn by the Spirit.

You move from I am who others perceive me to be, to I am who I am.

You move from using other people for their status to loving other people for their mystery.

You move from what am I going to do? To the essential question of who am I?

You move from making a name for yourself to humbly receiving your name from God.

You move from needing to be the point of life to the amazement that you are even a part of life.

You move from being over identified with the exterior to a deep living from the interior.

You move from a life of grasping for more to a life of living from grace.

While providing clarity on the second half of life, John Phillip Newell says, "It is about giving up our imaginary position as the center of the universe and finding that the true center is everywhere. It is about dying to to the way in which our ego, both individual and collective, tries stubbornly to be in charge, rather than faithfully, letting go to the Self who is within all selves."

It is telling in our culture that the concept of the second half of life is not more common.

To say there is not only more to life than the basic drives of the ego and cultural definitions of success is unwelcome. Stating that the real life we are seeking comes from the abandonment of the need for everything the dominant culture is telling you you're supposed to have to be happy is pure madness.

The vision of the second half of life is both countercultural and counterintuitive.

The freedom to be invisible is where you will be the most seen.

Not needing affirmation is where you will experience true validation

Everything is nothing, but in nothingness you will find everything.

Like I said. Madness.

So much of the first half of life is still willpower, gritting our teeth, and simply trying harder—even when we are using religious language as we do it. We're still overly concerned with winning, fixated on appearing successful, too easily seduced by power and those who occupy places of power, and still dangerously in awe of celebrity and status.

The main driving force is still about establishing your identity and using external forms of achievement and success to solidify a sense of self. The first half of life is still lacking depth in self-awareness, or lacking the courage to be true to the vision of the awareness they have received. This is because even if we have tasted the freedom of the true self, momentarily experienced our true self, and even use language of the true self, in the first half of life the ego is still spending the most time in the driver's seat.

At this point, your true self is more something you believe in, not yet something you have become.

I remember the first time I heard a story about a leader I respect burning out.

He shared about how he was heading toward a critical meltdown, but was unaware that it was coming. He talked about how he was losing all of his joy in his work, how he started to live with a great sense of fear of others, and how he was struggling to have the energy and imagination to create anything new.

He also showed how his deeper issues started to manifest themselves physically. He was having moments where it would be difficult to breathe, how his heart began to feel erratic at times, and even that his eyes stated twitching uncontrollably.

Eventually he would fully burnout—serotonin drained, adrenaline glands fried from being flooded by adrenaline for so long, and needing to build an entirely different future.

He was in his fifties when this happened, and despite how serious it was, I don't think this was the last burnout he would experience.

The energy for a life that grinds, grasps, strives, and works until burnout is always first half of life energy.

Second half of life energy that is drawn by the Spirit and flows naturally from who we are, accepts limitations freely. It moves into a mode of being that sees enjoying and rest as a central part of its life, and does not work until it burns out and gets sick.

There needs to be this evolutionary passage from the first to the second half of life, where we can shift from grinding and grasping to flowing at the pace of grace.

Make no mistake. While the journey between the first and second of life is connected, when you cross the threshold into the second half of life, it is a new path.

A path where the voice of comparison sounds like an almost unintelligible shouting from a distance, while we focus on whatever sacred task is in front of us.

A path where we have the freedom to stop fighting to establish our own personal greatness, and instead wake up to the beautiful mystery that everything we do subtly reverberates through the entire universe.

A path where we can live in awe because we see how our little corner of the universe is the very place where we experience the depth and fullness of life itself.

A path where we see enjoying as one of our primary tasks.

In the second half of life we move from believing to knowing, from seeing the journey to doing the journey, from receiving the love of

Jesus to living the life of Jesus, from believing in God to trusting in life, and to the profound discovery that we are home.

In the second half of life, you go from believing in God with your life to experiencing God as your life.

+ + +

I got my first recruitment letter for college basketball my sophomore year. As I was walking on campus, my basketball coach called me over to him and handed me a letter. The letter had bold lettering and a logo for Harvard. Because I was surprised and coming down from the weed that I smoked before school, I had to re-focus my senses as I opened the letter. So I calmly opened the envelope and proceeded to read. It was their basketball program telling me they were interested in me coming there to play basketball when I graduated in a few years.

As I finished reading the letter, I looked at the coach, cracked a smile and we both started laughing.

I started laughing because I had the feeling that if they knew what type of kid I was (which was expressed by how high I was while I was reading it), they might not be as interested in me.

I assumed he was laughing because he thought he same thing.

At sixteen years old, that letter represented the upward trajectory I was on in my basketball career. From that season, to camps, to AAU teams, to becoming one of the leading scorers in California my senior year, I was on a steady climb to being able to fulfill my dream of playing college basketball.

Through the disgustingly dry and hot summer days shooting hundreds of jump shots on the blacktop of my old elementary school, the endless amounts of hours I would walk through the streets of our city dribbling all alone, the sneaking into our high school gym to work out with no one around, I put myself in a position to play at high level.

My family and friends were proud, the public was aware of who I was and believed in where I was going, and it felt like a lot of eyes were on me.

During the last semester of my senior year of High School, a friend let me know that one of the better known drug dealers and users in our neighborhood wanted to have a meeting with me.

Which, as you can imagine, was a bit unsettling.

We had enough of a solid history together where I wasn't worried about the fact that he wanted to meet, but I may not have been one hundred percent relaxed walking into his house that day. I walked in, sat down on the couch and was immediately offered ten thousand dollars.

This offer was an investment in me because of the work I had been putting in and the name I was making for myself as a rapper. (That is too long of a story to tell here.)

By 18, I had recorded my first song, had a producer who was known and wanting to push me, and now had a local drug dealer who was wanting to help finance this next step of my process. I was in an ideal position to try and make the leap into a future in music most can only dream of.

I knew I had a life other people my age wanted.

I had gotten everything I had worked so hard for the previous four years, and I was standing at the threshold of taking the celebrity I had achieved locally to a larger scale and accomplishing all of my dreams.

And as I stood at the edge and looked out at the future I always dreamed of, what the culture tells you is where you will find real life, and that everyone who knew me expected me to step into,

I walked away from it all.

The clarity that emerged in my life from the light of Christ that had just been awakened within me a few months prior, enabled me to see and trust what I would hear Richard Rohr say five to seven years later,

"Life is not a matter of creating a special name for ourselves, but of uncovering the name we have always had."

Nobody understood, but I knew exactly what I was doing.

Nobody was there to guide me, but I knew exactly where I was going.

Nobody could confirm what I saw, but the light within made it impossible to not see.

One of the most terrifying parts of making the passage from your first to your second half of life is foreseeing what it is going to cost you.

The pastor at forty who knows if they were to be honest about where they are and how they view Jesus, the Bible, humanity, and life, it might cost them their congregation, and force them to start over.

The professional person in finance who understands that living truthfully might lead them to leaving their job, losing their high salary, and having to downsize their life.

The suburban mom of three who knows that if she were to fully own and communicate her more progressive social views, she would lose friendships, it would affect her kids' relationships, and it would introduce some unwanted complexity into her family's life.

This is where too many would be travelers to the second half of life get stuck.

We get close enough to the edge of the old where we start to have a broad vision of how

beautiful the second half of life is, but we also start to see what claiming this new territory will cost us. We get scared of what this evolutionary transition means for our life relationally, economically and socially.

This can be scary.

But the mystic and poet Hafiz says, "God is trying to sell you something, but you don't want to buy. That is what your suffering is: your fantastic haggling, your manic screaming over the price!"

I love that.

Our wrestling, suffering, and fighting is simply us desperately clinging to our small self, being scared to let go of the things that are no longer working, and clutching onto a life that we know is not real, but has been with us for so long that its hard to imagine life without it.

We fight the future the Spirit is inviting us into because we are unwilling to let go of a past that isn't even working.

Which is why, when referring to the experience of waking up, Thomas Merton writes, "…this awakening implies a kind of death to our exterior self, we will dread His coming in proportion as we are identified with this exterior self and attached to it."

The degree to which we are attached to our small self, is directly related to our refusal to accept the emergence of Christ and our true Self.

Human beings have a habit of holding on to the very things that get in the way of our freedom.

At eighteen, dying to my false self's project of establishing a name for itself meant that I had to walk away from both of these massive opportunities, and move on from the person who was known, admired, and celebrated.

Here's the thing.

I no longer loved basketball, I just needed it because of the status and value it gave me. I didn't want to make a career in music, it was just tempting because it allowed me to extend my ego's desire for celebrity. But now, I was no longer attached to the sense of self that made me well known to others because I had experienced the presence of God that made me who I actually am.

So after I graduated High School, I moved to Hawaii to explore a life in God, to be with my girlfriend, and to go to community college.

I quit playing basketball, I was no longer pursuing music, and I wasn't involved in the party scene because I was trying to get sober. I stopped doing everything I ever did to earn my worth based on manufactured forms, I was unknown and invisible to people, I had virtually nothing my ego could attempt to attach to for a sense of significance.

This is what the death of the first half of life self can feel like.

And this place of death that we naturally try and avoid at all costs became the space where the second half of my life could begin.

I was completely invisible, and felt seen for the first time.

I was a social nobody, and felt like myself more than ever.

I had no one applauding me anymore, and I felt more loved than I knew was even possible.

Every day I was invisible to those around me, I learned to trust that being seen by God is all I need. Every time I heard criticism from family, friends, and people I grew up with about the decision I made, I learned to surrender the need for the approval of others. Every moment I was tempted to tell people the story of my past as a way of making a name for myself (which I would fall back into some times), I quietly received my name and life from God. Every morning I woke up knowing I was going to get zero applause from anyone, which meant each day was a fresh opportunity to relinquish that need, relax into my true self, and rest in that simple but sacred feeling of being me.

Out of this emptiness, my own voice could emerge.

Out of the death of my insecure self, authenticity was birthed.

Out of the sacrifice of who I thought I was, I was born again as who I am.

+ + +

Sometimes when we cannot get the feel for an experience, it is good to see the fruit of the experience. Seeing the practical outworking of a transformative event, can open us up the actual event. So, let's talk a little bit about some of the unique fruit that will naturally bare in the second half of life.

The second half of life does not work until burnout.

Burnout is fueled by a lack of trusting in our inherent value, an avoidance of vulnerability, an obsession with a form of success that is only born out of the ego, a refusal to feel our feelings, and the need to hustle for our worth.

The self that is grounded in Christ and knows who it is never works until burnout.

The Self that believes it is enough would never push itself physically or overextend itself emotionally—which leads to burnout—because it is simply not in its nature to do so. Burnout makes no sense to the Self that trusts the conclusion of its own value. Only the insecure and small self of the first half of life would ever do that to themselves.

The second half of life abandons any notion of a tit for tat universe.

This self does not need every event to make sense or to fit them into a controllable worldview, and it does not have to be able to explain pain and suffering because it has cultivated the inner capacity to hold creative tension, to carry paradox, and to simply allow reality to be.

There does not have to be a need for a clearly defined cause and effect relationship in the universe in order to see it as essentially good. In the second half of life, you know that beneath the surface of airtight logical systems, rigid apologetics, and the need to understand why every single thing happens is just the ego's need for control. And in the second half of life, the need for control no longer has the power to lead you, even if you're able to hear it calling you.

The second half of life knows what it wants.

To add to this, in the second half of life, we know what we want, because we know who we are and accept who we're not. In this more quiet, settled, and spacious space, we can tell the difference between what we want and what others want for us.

This Self has developed the clarity of who it is and the sensitivity to the Spirit to know the difference between what desires in me have been planted there by others, and what desires are authentic to me.

In the second half of life, we are no longer trying to do everything in order to not miss out on life, we are instead giving ourselves to the one or two things that are ours to do, and tasting all of life through those specific areas.

In the second half of life we can enjoy.

The Self that has finally transcended the ego and all of its superficial needs, and has been liberated from its need to prove and establish itself, can simply enjoy.

The language and experiences of striving, struggling, and grasping are replaced by the experiences of wonder, embrace, and appreciation. The world no longer feels like something out there to try and fight and overcome because it has been transfigured into something we participate in, marvel at, and enjoy.

And of course, it's not actually the world out there that has been transfigured is it?

There's a ground of joy that is held together through the necessary tears shed along the way.

There's an anchor of peace that transcends our own individual life that is our true center.

There's a flow of freedom that has nothing to do with the events of our personal life that we settle into and move forward in.

There's a relaxed, vast, uncoiled, and immense space we live from that has been opened up through transcending, overcoming, letting go, allowing, relinquishing, accepting, and merging with the unified field.

Of course.

Because there is the first half of life and there is the second half of life.

THE PRODUCT AND THE PROCESS

There are times when the creative life feels like a great gift and other times it feels like a great burden.

Its powerful when you're imagining, creating, and coming up with ideas and the creative threads of life seem to weave together in and through you.

There are other times when you just got an unexpected and disappointing email, you heard what someone else said about you or your work and you are jolted with anxiety. You feel stuck or things seem to keep falling apart as you put them back together, and you aren't sure how much longer you can do this.

Some of you just thought, "yes, I know that feeling, it's called Wednesday afternoon."

Why is that?

Why at times does the creative life feel like a gift and why sometimes does it feel like an impossible burden?

Why sometimes does creative work seem to take weight off of you and other times actually seems to put weight on you?

Why are you excited to start, and why at other times do you question whether you should have even started this in the first place?

In Mark 4, Jesus tells a story about a farmer scattering seed. Jesus said:

> "This is what the kingdom of God is like. A man scatters seed on the ground. Night and day, whether he sleeps or gets up, the seed sprouts and grows, though he does not know how. All by itself the soil produces grain—first the stalk, then the head, then the full kernel in the head. As soon as the grain is ripe, he puts the sickle to it, because the harvest has come."

The funny thing about this story is that any farmer today and everybody in Jesus' first century agrarian society would say, "That's not how you do that!"

There is a significantly more complex process that enables agricultural growth, and almost comedically more precision required to guide this process. You can not just scatter seed haphazardly, sleep in, sporadically check on the crops, and assume you are going to have an abundant harvest to gather at the end. On a practical level, this makes no sense to someone who knows you need to have a lot more control of the process in order to guarantee your desired outcome.

According to Jesus, this is what the Kingdom of God is like.

So, in the Kingdom of God and the economy of grace, growing and creating looks a bit different than what we are used to.

So what do we see here?

The person has their role.

They have the courage to begin, the initiative to take, and their own unique process.

But there is also the surrender, the embrace of the mystery, and the acceptance that ultimately they are not in control. The man scatters his seed, and then he lets go and allows the pace of grace to guide the affairs.

He demonstrates that it's not about having control of the process, it's about having courage in the present.

+ + +

Whether it is crafting sermons, preparing classes, creating scripts for short films, or writing this book, my experience creating is substantially different than the experience of people who see and consume the end product.

The sermon they hear on a Sunday had a Monday through Saturday.

The film they see included writing, editing, recording, and shooting.

This book you're reading was written on a love seat, with a side table for a desk, in my bedroom during quarantine (which is probably why my back hurts now).

There is the process and there is the product.

And one of the most vital discoveries I have made through creating is this:

The product is for others, but the process is for you.

While existentially, we can talk about the inherent joy of existence itself, creatively, we must also realize the inherent joy of creation itself. It is so easy to create with the unconscious assumption that creating means we give some kind of offering in order to get something back from the world.

I provide this, I get paid money.
I create this, I get applause.
I build this, I get recognition.

If we operate with this transactional imagination as the ground of all of our creative life, we will forever be bound to the opinions, views, and responses of others.

If I get what I want, I live,
If I do not get what I want, I die.

Sounds extreme, but this is how it feels to the ego.

If we know the inherent joy of creation itself, this transactional relationship is undone, and an entirely new way of creating is born. We see that one of the great paradoxes of life is that the gift is actually in the giving.

It's not, what do I get from what what I give?

It's the surprising realization that what I get is hidden within the sacred act of giving itself.

My joy is in the crafting that happens Monday though Saturday. The greatest gift I receive from the giving is being fully present in the giving. When I'm creating, writing, and giving myself, I'm not worried about what I am going to get from it, because everything I want emerges as my very life as I am giving it.

The mystic is not trying to be grateful for the gifts in life, the mystic is trusting and grateful for the gift of life. Which also means the greatest gifts do not come from creating, they are experienced through creating.

It's this exciting and joy filled experience that Steve McIntosh writes about when he says that, "The rising flow of creativity that has given birth to our universe is coursing within us at this very moment."

Here, the boundaries between giving and getting, offering and outcomes, and the product and the process start to fade, and eventually dissolve because we have transcended the transactional imagination of the ego, and have subtly entered into the realm of gift.

We are creating out of the realm of gift when we are fully present, wholly engaged, and completely free from worrying about the outcomes.

You can always tell when people are not creating out of the realm of gift because they are still operating out of a tit for tat universe as they create. Their hearts are still caught in the old game of return on investment, reward and punishment, expressing and expectations, and as a result, they miss all of the ways how their heart can open and how their spirit can relax through creating itself.

This is why Abraham Joshua Heschel said, "There is joy in the love of labor, but misery in the love of gain."

The joy is in the process.

The burden is obsessing over outcomes.

The truth is that we do not stay in the pure space of gift all of the time while we are creating and working. And to break down these differences between gift or burden as a simple binary of either/or would not do the complexity of our relationship with creativity justice.

It is more accurate to see gift and burden as two separate ends of the same scale we fluidly move back and forth on during the act of creating.

Sometimes we are closer to the side of gift. When we are here, the joy and flow of creating makes up our inner atmosphere. In other moments we slide closer to the burden end of the scale. When this takes place, anxiety and heaviness cling to us as if we have no say in the matter.

Which raises an important question.

What if there's a way to get some clarity on where we are in this scale, why we are there, and some hints to listen to that can help us recognize our location and slide closer to the end of gift?

If there is, maybe we can be aware and free enough to move into the heart of gift, to recover the joy of creating, and to rediscover again and again that the getting is actually in the giving.

+ + +

When you are operating out of gift, the questions you ask when you begin are, who am I and what do I want to make? When you are getting closer to burden, the questions you begin with are, who are they, and what are they going to like?

These grounding questions to our work not only determine the degree of joy we are going to experience, they also regulate the degree to which our work flows out of the truth of who we are.

This starting point of the creative process is about authenticity vs. artificiality, knowing your value vs. letting others determine your value, creating from the inside out vs. creating from the outside in.

Gift is about knowing who you are and owning your voice.

When you are a pastor, a leader, or a kind of guide for people, one of the greatest resources you have to offer people is availability. As a person who makes availability a central part of your being and doing, you end up having all kinds of interesting conversations with people.

I've surfed with people and sat in the water in-between waves, and heard stories about absentee dads, and the role music and the church played in their life in during this absence.

I've had drinks at a bar with a gay man from our church who directly asked me why I care about him or the spiritual health of people in the LGBTQ community.

I've sat around tables of coffee shops with creatives discussing authenticity, creativity, and how it is so much harder to keep going than most people would ever realize.

Through all of these relationships, connections, and conversations, one of the questions I consistently ask that seems like a hard one for people to answer is:

What do you want?

It is astounding how difficult it can be for so many people to answer that one defining and clarifying question. What do you want?

Of course, it's hard to know what you want when you don't know who you are.

Creatively, we begin with owning our voice, and that is made possible by knowing who we are and what our unique voice actually sounds like.

When we start creating something, the natural reaction of the ego is to start with asking,

What should I say?
What do they think will be good?
What will they like?

This question immediately creates a low level anxiety and establishes a creative path that mutes authenticity. It also is the beginning point for any creative project to be held together by fear, which will inevitably become a burden we carry within, and a weight we carry on us.

The real questions do not begin with who others are and what they want, they begin with who we are and what we want.

Who am I?
What do I want to create?
What do I genuinely believe about this?

Based on the unique make up of who I am, the depth of wisdom I draw upon, and the dynamic presence of the Spirit within, I begin with my own desire and my own vision. This beginning point opens up a wide space for who I am to authentically emerge.

This makes the process feel light.

This is the key that unblocks the door to gift, and liberates us to walk down this creative journey in such a way where it feels like the weight of life is falling off us as we create.

Einstein said, "Be a voice, not an echo."

Our own voice is heard when we are operating out of gift, and we slowly settle into being an echo when we allow fear and the desires of others to draw us closer to burden.

+ + +

Gift creates joy and flow, while burden creates stress and anxiety.

Gift takes weight off you, while burden places weight on you.

This is why one simple way to gauge whether you are closer to the edge of gift or burden is by paying attention to the weight you are carrying, and what inner experience the act of creating is producing in you.

When the creative process feels heavier, produces anxiety and worry, and the inherent joy seems too good to be true, you are probably sliding closer to burden.

When the experience feels lighter, yields excitement and appreciation, and the inherent joy becomes present, you are more than likely sliding toward gift.

Let's talk about flow.

One of the defining factors of being in a flow state is "Transient Hypofrontality." This means that while you're in that creative flow, there is a temporary deactivation of your prefrontal cortex, which is the part of the brain charged with self-monitoring. When this happens, it's like your inner critic that judges and analyzes what you're doing goes silent and you're able to create in a very uninhibited way.

(Thank you Mihaly Csikszentmihalyi for introducing me to this.)

Most of the time, this experience seems to be random.

But awareness of what is happening within you while you are creating and learning how to dis-identify with outcomes and expectations of others, means the joy that comes with the flow state does not have to be allusive and sporadic. It can actually become a more consistent ground to stand on as you create.

It is said that Picasso could paint for hours and hours without any fatigue, and that his ability to be present in this process was much more valuable to him than the response to the final product.

After over thirty years in the music industry and making over a billion dollars, Dr. Dre stays creative, engaged, and alive as an artist because of his simple and steadfast commitment to the craft of his art as a producer.

Writing, creating, crafting, and making the connections during my own process of making is what brings me the greatest joy, allows me to lose track of the duration of time that passes, and keeps me in love with what I do.

(I added myself because I'm the only one who would ever put my name near Picasso and Dr. Dre in print.)

The inherent joy of creating exists within a great paradox:trying to control outcomes creates anxiety, which inhibits imaginative capacity. But surrendering outcomes creates flow, which unleashes imaginative capacity.

So the more you try and control the outcome, the more anxious you will be, and the less likely you will create the outcome you desire. And the more you let go of the outcome, the more spacious you will feel, which means the more likely you are to create the desired outcome.

Letting go of control of the future liberates you to to create the future.

When all of the value of something is contingent on the response of others, how can you not be worried and anxious?

+ + +

Gift gives birth to the experience of "I can't believe I get to do this."
While burden creates the experience of "I just want to get through
this."

For the first three to four years of Imagine, we would meet for
worship on Sunday nights. While gathering at night for our church
was the best thing those first few years, it also made Sundays
extremely challenging for me personally.

The entire day was a slow, steady, and uncomfortable build up to
the night.

I would go on an early morning walk to organize, talk out loud,
and start to memorize or internalize my teaching. I would come
home, work on slides of the visuals for the teaching, rest a little bit,
make sure everything and everyone was together for that night,
and then I would go on one more walk outside to go over my
teaching again.

And I live in Hawaii.

And it's always hot outside.

So, yes, I would be sweating every time I got back to the house.

So, as this low level, anticipatory anxiety would be present and
growing in my body throughout the day, it would always sit in my
stomach and make it slightly upset, and drain my energy levels.

(Nerves have always affected me this way. Which is why when I
played football as a kid, right before a game when my teammates

would get pumped up and want to bang helmets with each other, whenever they came to me, I would be like, "no thanks," because my upset stomach and low energy would have made me into a practice dummy in that moment.)

And there would always be this moment at 3:30 pm, knowing a couple guys were coming to my house at 4 pm to load up their truck, where I would stop, look at the beautiful chase on my couch and think, "I can't wait to get through this, come home to you, pour a glass of wine, and watch Netflix."

I would have that exact thought, "I can't wait to get through this."

In that situation, all I could feel was the discomfort in my body, all I could see was how much energy I still had to exert, which meant all I could think about was trying to get through.

But think about that statement.

I can't wait to get through this.

Get through what?

You want to get through the one thing you are committing your life to? You want to just get through the amazing chance to do what you love, knowing that the words you share have the power to open up new worlds for people? You want to simply get through being able to help create a space for people to experience the light, to encounter the love, and to get a glimpse of the Christ that holds all things together?

To do what?

Be at home having a glass of wine while you're exhausted and barely able to open your eyes?

And every time I would feel that temptation to treat this gift like a burden and devalue it by seeing it as something to get through, I would smile to myself, and move forward with a deep sense of gratitude and joy.

(Okay. Not every time.)

Each time was like a fresh epiphany of knowing this is not something I have to get through, this is something I get to give myself too. To be present to what a gift it is I'm doing and to be awake to the divine electricity of the universe we're all plugged into. To be alive to the people around me and the words that flow through me. And to be grateful that I am doing something that not only grounds me in joy personally, but also opens up the possibility of joy in our community.

The joy is in the making.
The gift is in the giving.
The life is in the creating.

Joy knows that it's always about giving ourselves to the next thing we're going to make, knowing the next thing is never going to make us.

FEELING SHITTY

Sometimes you are going to feel shitty.

On a slow Wednesday afternoon, where you are in disbelief about how little you accomplished during the day, and begin thinking about where you are creatively and with work as a whole.

On a long drive in between the barrage of meetings, conversations, and errands where you have space to think about everything you are doing to hold together all of the pieces of your life, and begin having that unexpected moment when you're asking if any of it even matters.

On a Monday when you felt particularly inspired to take some steps forward and then get caught in a mindless scroll through Instagram and you end up in that overwhelming place of comparison again.

Sometimes you are going to feel shitty.

And that's okay.

And not only is it okay to feel shitty, but each time you find yourself thrown into this uncomfortable experience, there is actually an opening into the light of God, and an opportunity for a deeper trust in your essential Self. If we do not avoid or distract ourselves from these feelings, and let our selves be present to them, we will discover that right there in the middle of that shitty feeling, there is an invitation to a further freedom waiting in Christ.

I can remember one specific Monday morning during the first two years of starting Imagine, where I woke up and life just felt heavy. I could feel the tension in my body between where I was and where I thought I should be, and I felt shitty.

At one level during these moments, it seems as if there is almost no particular trigger for why things feel heavier, or no way to identify one concrete circumstance that has made you feel this way.

Sometimes you just feel shitty.

But quite often, the truth is that if you sit with that feeling long enough and allow it to have a voice, there is going to be clarity about the connection between the thoughts and beliefs you are having and the emotion you are feeling.

For me on that Monday morning, it was:

Does any of this even matter? Do people actually care about Imagine? A part of me worries that if my friends and supporters knew exactly where the church was at this point, they would be disappointed. Our church should be further along than where it is right now. Sometimes I feel like an idiot for really trying, because I never want to be the fool who really cares about something that others are indifferent too.

During these uninvited spaces in our life, the condemning thoughts we have are always repetitive and playing by similar rules, because ultimately they're all a part of the same ego games.

Does this matter? I should be further than where I am. Can I keep going? Does anyone actually care about my contribution to this world?

Because beneath the surface of all of these specific questions, it's actually just one question.

Is what I'm doing enough?

Now, on that Monday morning when I was feeling shitty and having all of these thoughts barge into my mind, I could feel something else begin to happen within me. In the midst of this uncomfortable feeling and these unwanted thoughts, there was this other voice I could hear coming from the contraction of my ego that was saying,

"You should be doing more. Pay attention! Here is an idea! What you need to do is launch something brand new that looks just like this!"

And all of the sudden I could see this exciting new idea, of which the details and plan just seemingly started to naturally unfold in my imagination. I could see it, and it was a great idea, and it was so vivid, it was as if I was already living in it. And during that little imaginative trip of what could possibly be the future of our church, I realized something:

This new idea was distracting me from feeling my feelings and facing the truth.

And to extend that even further, this new idea that was spontaneously arising from my ego was not only an unconscious way of avoiding the painful and uncomfortable emotions I was feeling, it was also a way to overcompensate for the condemning thoughts I was having. During that imaginative trip into the future this great idea was taking me on, not only was I distracted from my feelings, I was also starting to convince myself that I would, in fact, be doing enough if this idea came to fruition.

Sometimes when you are thinking of all of the things wrong with your work and your life, and you somehow naturally start planning and preparing for a new thing, that immediate impulse to come up with next better thing is often an unconscious attempt to try and achieve your way out of feelings of inadequacy.

(It's amazing to think how often pastor's impulses for new "mission" campaigns or church projects are actually a way for them to avoid feeling hard emotions and facing themselves with honesty in those unbearable Monday morning moments.)

Here is what all of this builds toward and hopefully enables us to see with more clarity. Every time we are feeling like this about our work and lost in that vortex of justification, condemning thoughts, and uncomfortable emotions, what we are truly asking is am I doing enough?

And even further beneath the surface than that, what we are really really asking is, am I enough?

We think it's about performance, but it's actually about identity.

We think it's about vocation, but it's always about value.

We think it's about whether or not what we are doing enough, when it's essentially about whether or not we believe we are enough.

It's not just the shitty feeling we avoid, it's what we believe our lack of progress says about our core value that we are unable to accept. It's not just the painful moment we can't accept, it's what we think this moment means about who we are that is too much for us to face. If we cannot convince ourselves that we are doing enough, we are unable to believe that we are enough.

The questions you're asking about your performance are only answered through trusting who you are in God's presence.

This is why these spaces of struggle always have the potential to become unexpected openings into the heart of Christ. Whenever you are wrestling with vocation, value, identity, and are asking the question, 'Am I doing enough?' There are two ways to respond.

The first one is by convincing yourself you are doing enough through internal argument and justification, or by planning some new project or idea that, if completed, will be the thing that will solidify that you are doing enough. Which may allow you to hold onto the illusion of performance based value a little longer.

The second is to hold that uncomfortable space of emotion, refuse to do anything out of the impulses of your ego, and receive the moment as opening to surrender further into and to relax in that always available open space of grace.

This where you learn how to let yourself feel shitty.

Instead of avoiding your feelings and throwing yourself into the next project to prove to yourself that you're enough based on what you're doing, you need to feel your feelings, and stay open long enough to experience God's presence enough so you can know you are enough based on who you are. This means that while you are feeling shitty and tempted to perform better, work harder, and do more to prove to yourself that you are doing enough, there's another way to respond.

You can uncoil and relax into the open space of Spirit,
You can rest in the simple feeling of being you.
You can turn and receive the eternal gaze from God that is pure affirmation.

This is where you know and experience for yourself what the great mystic St. Catherine of Sienna discovered, "I cannot lose anything in the place of abundance I have found."

Experiencing unconditional love and affirmation when the circumstances of your life are persuading you that you are not doing enough and making you feel shitty…is everything.

You can allow yourself to feel shitty because there is a deeper part of you that is "hidden with God in Christ" (Col. 3:8) that knows who you are. You just have to refuse to be busy, to feel those feelings, and see that when you hold that space long enough, you can collapse into your true self.

It is here, you realize what Richard Rohr meant when he said, "suddenly this is a very safe universe. You have nothing to be afraid of. God is for you. God is leaping toward you! God is on your side, honestly more than you are on your own."

Each of these moments when you're feeling kind of shitty about your work can be received as an invitation from God to trust even more in who He says you are in the immediacy of your heart. And each time you avoid this feeling to do more in order to prove you are enough to yourself, you miss that opening and opportunity from God to trust that you are already that which you're trying prove.

It's not about achieving for others it's about acceptance from God.
It's not about working more, it's about waking up.
It's not about trying harder, it's about trusting more.

It's not about fleeing from those negative emotions by climbing higher, it's about falling though those negative emotions by knowing that the ground you fall on is made of grace.

Only the person who trusts they're enough has the freedom to let themselves feel shitty—because they know that no matter what critical thoughts are present within that shitty feeling, those intruders say absolutely nothing about who they are. It's the one who is unable to trust they are enough who can not embrace the freedom to feel shitty, because of the underlying fear that this feeling is in fact, who they are.

So back to my original story.

As I laid on my couch feeling shitty on that Monday morning, here's what I did—I just let myself feel shitty for a while. I refused to play the game where I present my case in the internal courtroom to prove I'm dong enough. I resisted the temptation to throw myself into the next big project in order to avoid my feelings. I simply felt the feelings, allowed all of those thoughts to come and go, and I opened my heart long enough to trust and receive the one thing directly from God that we keep trying to grind for outside of God. Which is the simple and sacred experience of being enough.

Pay attention.

Just beneath the surface, our life is always asking "Am I enough?" And in specific moments, if you let yourself feel shitty long enough, and keep your heart open wide enough, you might just wake up to the love of God within who keeps insisting that you are.

OBSERVING THINGS TO DEATH

Guilt and shame weigh a lot.

I have witnessed them bother, pull down, and sometimes even crush people who are close to me. They stick to people, they haunt people, they follow people around wherever they go, and they seem to be quite stubborn when it comes to trying to get rid of them.

Another irritating part of these two is that they do not just answer the door whenever the mistakes that we make start knocking, they barge into the living room of people's lives even when they don't like the thoughts people are having.

Have you ever felt guilty for thoughts that you have?

Have you ever felt shame because of the first reaction you have to a situation, even though the reaction stays in your mind?

Do you ever hear the offering of guilt from your inner critic and end up not just with the guilt, with some anger to go with it? And now you're frustrated with yourself because you can't seem to beat your inner critic, and still allow it to have so much power over you?

Which of course, then leads to an ongoing cycle of guilt, anger, and frustration that you can't seem to out maneuver in the court room of your own mind? Do you ever catch yourself fighting or avoiding certain thoughts you have, or attempting to wrestle them into submission through willpower or justification only to end up exhausted, discouraged, and defeated by the end?

If you answer yes to any of these questions or connect with the general struggle expressed here, you are not alone, and it doesn't always have to be this way.

Here's the thing.

We can assume we are our thoughts.

This means it can be so easy to be over identified with the mind that we have a hard time distinguishing between who we are and the thoughts we have.

The phrase "train of thought" exists, and is so accurate because thoughts are like trains that come through our mind, call us to get on board, and almost force us to respond obediently by going wherever they take us. Sometimes, it can feel like we do not even have a choice.

There is a difference between having thoughts and our thoughts having us.

This is true for our emotions too.

In the same way we can assumed we are our thoughts, we also can feel we are our feelings.

You can see this based on how we talk about our feelings when we are experiencing them. When someone is upset, you are probably not going to hear them say, "I am having intense feelings of anger right now!"

No.

What they will more than likely say is, "I am so angry right now."

To say I am angry is not to identify an emotion you have, it is to say that the anger is actually who you are in the moment. It is challenging for us to separate our thoughts and the emotions we have from who we are.

Just recently, I told my daughter to go to the bathroom before we went somewhere.

I actually told her she needs to go potty.

Right as I finished the sentence, she tried to finesse me and explain why it was unnecessary for her to do so. But, before she could finish, I interrupted and said, "Mikayla, you need to go potty right now."

To which she hilariously replied, "Uuuuuggghhhhh! I am upset right now!"

It was one of those moments you need to hold firm boundaries as a parent while you try and keep from laughing.

Do you see? She did not say she had feelings of anger or being upset, she completely identified with them because in that moment she actually was them. (Let's give her another developmental break here.) But this is the important thing.

You are not your thoughts.
You are not your feelings.
You have thoughts, and you have feelings.

You feel guilty when you have vindictive thoughts because you think you are vindictive. You cannot overcome the power of your inner critic because without the necessary separation from your thoughts, you don't have an inner critic that speaks from a distance, you are the inner critic that communicates with your very own voice. You feel a sense of shame and want to beat yourself up because of a mistake you made, because instead of being a person who made a mistake, you immediately feel like you are the mistake itself.

How do we think about our thinking differently, and what are we supposed to feel when it comes to our feelings?

Those are both weird questions.

But they are important ones.

+ + +

In contemplation, one of the central things that is happening is that you are dis-identifying with your ego, and differentiating from your mind.

While referring to what is happening during silence and meditation, Steve McIntosh describes "…meditation as a process for liberating the practitioner's consciousness from identification with the stream of thoughts that usually occupy the mind."

Silence, solitude, and the relaxed, uncoiled, and open space of contemplation give you enough room to experience your true Self. It is also in this process you directly realize that whoever you are is before, beneath, and beyond your thoughts, emotions, and impulses. Through this inner spaciousness of contemplation, you experience the space between your true Self and the ego and its desires, and the distance between who you are and the thoughts you have.

In contemplation, you realize you are not the thoughts you have, you are the space within which those thoughts arise.

It is here you experientially discover that anything that can be seen by you is not you, and that any thought, emotion, or desire that arises in your awareness is separate from you because you are, in fact, the awareness itself. You are never that which can be seen because you are the one who is doing the seeing. So, in this contemplative stance, what we experience sounds and feels like this:

I am over here having thoughts that are over there.
I am over here having feelings that are separate from me.
I am over here having desires that are not who I am.
There is the I. There is the arising. There is the distance between.

This is how we make that transformative move from looking through our thoughts and emotions to looking at them, which is the beginning of being liberated from them.

There were a lot of people who were critical of me, and there were a lot of horrible things said about me when I walked away from all my opportunities at eighteen and moved to Hawaii. I moved to completely give my life to seeking God, to try to get sober, and to be with my girlfriend who was already in Hawaii, and most of what people said about this decision was not very nice.

I remember going to a family function before I left for Hawaii, and one of my little cousins who was seven or eight years old, came up to me and said,

"My daddy told me you're throwing everything away just to follow some girl to Hawaii."

To which I replied,

"Well is your daddy around right now? Because I'm about to whoop your little ass…"

Okay, I didn't actually say that, but I may have been thinking and imagining something like that!

But even with family saying things about my decision, the words that affected me the most came from the friends and peers I grew up with. Because I still stayed close to a couple friends, I kept my ear to the streets enough to be able to hear what "they" were saying.

"Kevin's a little bitch for leaving the neighborhood."

"He's a dumbass for not trying to go further in music."

"He's gonna regret what he did, that relationship is not going to last and he'll be back here within a year."

At eighteen or nineteen, in my new dorms in Hawaii, I remember so vividly how offended and upset I would start to feel. And as I felt that anger arise, I would start to imagine what I would do to some of these people when I came home for Christmas break, and I would have this dialogue in my head about what would happen between us.

But soon after that anger and offense started arising I would stop, step back in my imagination, watch all of those thoughts, look at all of those feelings, and start to ask myself questions.

Why does it matter what they think? Who cares what they are saying? Is your sense of self still attached to how others perceive you? I thought this new Self we are living into means we are moving beyond that. It's okay for them to think that. Their opinions do not change anything about the essence of who you are.

They don't see what you see because they haven't experienced what you've experienced.

And as I observed those thoughts and feelings, I would begin to gain distance from them, start to dis-identify with them, and ultimately transcend them and rest in the open space of the Spirit and my Self.

Anytime you look at something, you have enough space to recognize that the thought, emotion, or object is not actually you. It may be arising within you, but it is not you.

Anytime you look at something, you momentarily dis-identify with it, which is the beginning point for ultimately transcending it.

We have to remember.

This is not a conceptual belief, it is a directly realized and immediately liberating experience of knowing that the you that is hidden in Christ, is distinct from any and all of the thoughts, emotions, and desires of the ego and the false self. This is where you know you are not your thoughts, you have thoughts. When you realize you are not your emotions, you have emotions. That you are not the desires of the ego, but rather are the wide open space that makes room for all of this to arise within you, and ultimately pass right by you.

In reference to the passing nature of all thoughts emotions or objects arising in your own awareness, Ken Wilber writes, "But what does not come or go is your own pure witness, or True Seer, or unmovable Real Self."

Unmovable Real Self.

Yes.

So, when the writer in Hebrews 6 talks about the anchor of the soul being firm and secure, they are speaking of the Self that is distinct from and exists beyond anything that is arising within or passing through your awareness.

The Self is centered, anchored, and a fixed, yet transcendent point.

Everything else
arises within it,

passes by it,
moves through it,
and remains distinct from it.

Without contemplation, we will never experience enough distance from our ego, which means we will always be too attached to our ego, which ultimately means we will never be freed from our ego.

+ + +

One of the main reasons people get stuck in their minds, anxious from their thinking, and end up attached to their thoughts is because they are always judging their thoughts, desires, and feelings.

I can't think that because that's wrong.

I can't have that thought because its inappropriate (these are usually the funniest though!).

I can't want that because good people are not supposed to want that.

When we are in a steady flow of judging our thoughts, we are inevitably going to be caught up in an endless wrestling match with our thoughts.

We will try and deny them or avoid them, we will consistently be trying to justify them or explain them, or we will try and fight them and overcome with our own strength and force (which never works). Every time we try and fight our mind or overpower our ego, we actually reinforce it and make it stronger, which ultimately leaves it having more power over us than it had to begin with.

Whenever you judge something, you are not able to simply let it be.

This is why we need to learn the art of nonjudgmental awareness.

One of the easiest things to say, one of the hardest things to do.

Nonjudgmental awareness allows each and every thought and desire you have to simply be exactly what it is.

It does not need to explain it, justify it, deny it, avoid it, or label it good or bad. It simply allows the thought to be what it is, and to have its place in the stream of your consciousness.

The first step in being more freed from your thoughts is seeing them with nonjudgmental awareness. To see the ego for what it is, recognize the desires as they arise, and allow them to be without trying to fight them, justify them, or explain them.

Nonjudgmental awareness paves a path to freedom beyond our thoughts, feelings, and our ego impulses.

Nonjudgmental awareness allows everything to arise naturally and calmly in your awareness. If something painful or a thought you normally would judge arises, you just let it arise. You don't have to judge it and not accept it, decide it's too painful and avoid it, attempt to fight it and overcome it, or react to the impulse to justify it.

You simply allow it to arise, understand that it is not you, hold it in your awareness without turning away, feel it begin to lose its grip on you, and rest in that vast open space of Spirit, knowing that love is more powerful than whatever arises.

The thought or desire arises, you observe it, hold that uncomfortable space in your body, slowly watch it lose its power over you, and then let it go and fall back into your presence in the presence of God.

This is what I call observing things to death.

+ + +

I was at a coffee shop with a young man from our church. I was probably about thirty at the time, and he was around twenty three.

This was a kid I liked, whose presence at Imagine I appreciated, and someone whose creative work I respected tremendously. So, when it came to the arts, he was a person whose perspective I was always interested in and intrigued by.

During that conversation, as we were covering a broad spectrum of topics, somehow my teaching became the topic. He proceeded to tell me that during the first six months of Imagine, every single one of my teachings was mind blowing to him.

Revelatory.
Paradigm Shifting.
Consciousness altering.

Okay, maybe that is not verbatim, but he was getting there!

Then he told me that after the first six months, these last three to four teachings I did before we were going to move into our public space—not so much. He did not have the same experience, did not see them as unique or powerful as the others, and simply was not as impressed or moved by them.

Okay.

Cool.

Glad we had this talk.

In that moment I could feel my ego contract and get slightly offended for about ten to twenty seconds, as the conversation quickly moved on.

After we were done hanging out, I got in my car, started driving away, thought of that moment, and decided to pull over to sit with it for a moment. I acknowledged the slight offense, and recognized that the only thing that was offended was that little part of my ego that wants people to think highly of my teaching. So I let go of that need, surrendered the moment to the Spirit, and then simply moved on.

That process was probably two to three minutes.

Within that moment of feeling that first offense, there were easily three to five ridiculous thoughts that came up within me and floated along my stream consciousness.

"I take time out of my day to kick it with this kid, and he wants to critique my teaching?"

"He doesn't even understand that I have a role to lead people throughout this transition, he doesn't get it."

"Definitely not going to hang with him anymore, probably won't even be as cool with him after."

"I'm over this kid."

(I will stop there for the sake of humiliation.)

These kinds of ridiculous thoughts are just reactions of the ego that are not who you actually are. They are uncontrollable thoughts that arise within you that you do not have to identify with.

But, it was only because I could allow those thoughts to arise within a nonjudgmental space, knowing they were simply uncontrollable reactionary quips, that I was able to sit with the event, observe it to death, and process it so quickly. If I were to judge those thoughts and repress them, the offended energy of the moment would go into my shadow and I would not be able to let it go.

The thoughts arise. I observe them, name them, then see what is really going on, and then I can move on. But without the initial allowing of the thoughts to arise, I would have never been able to let them go.

One of the biggest surprises people will discover is that the foundation for so much transformation is the simple and subtle act of observation. When the ego is speaking loudly, when the desires of the ego arise, when our thoughts are saying and doing things we do not want to become, we must resist the urge to deny them, avoid them, or fight them.

Although it sounds overly simplified, what we need to do is just observe them.

The thought or desire arises, and as we see it within the space of our awareness, we hold it long enough, and as we allow it space, eventually it will be exhausted of its strength, and in the end, will have no power left over us.

It is not fighting, resisting, or rejecting,

It is observing, allowing, and accepting.

This internal movement of allowing anything to arise with no judgment, and without needing to react to every impulse that emerges in your awareness is not only a sign of freedom, it is the clearest path to freedom.

You cannot be freed from what you will not face.

The good news is that you do not have to turn away from anything that makes itself known in your awareness, because nothing we can see is who we are. No desire, no thought, no shameful memory, no expression of the ego can withstand the presence of love, or overcome the power of God.

Our great Self is not the things that arise within us, it is the sacred space,
extraordinary emptiness,
holy horizon,
and amazing awareness itself.

We are not each and every plane that lands on or takes off on the runway of our consciousness, we are the runway itself.

RELIGION AND REALITY

"Do you want to meet and get a drink?"

This was the question an old friend of mine from Los Angeles asked me while he was visiting Hawaii, after he called me in a slightly panicked state.

And because one, I like the guy who called me, and two, I like beer, I responded with the most confident yes I could give as a pastor. About forty five minutes later, we were sitting down at a bar in Waikiki, and he proceeded to fill me in on what just happened.

Right before he called me, he found out he was getting laid off.

He was hurt, surprised, overwhelmed, and his body responded with this sense of shock that left him virtually frozen.

He said as soon as he got the news, he turned on some worship music in his AirPods, went on his balcony and started reading the Bible so he could distract himself from his thoughts and feelings.

Interesting.

The worship music was a distraction.

The words from Jesus prevented him from facing the truth.

The sacred stories that can connect us to God became a way to evade feeling his own life.

Now, this is no judgment toward him—I understand the unconscious seeking of any form of relief when we get triggered with something painful—but it demonstrates how easy it is for people to use religion as a way to avoid feeling and facing the truth.

It's easy for religion to be used as a way of avoiding reality.

You can perform all the right rituals and never learn to be real with God.

You can sing and shout as loud as you can and never be honest about the pain you are carrying.

You can use the name of Jesus incessantly, while hiding from the vulnerability, emotional risk, and openheartedness that is required to love people like Christ.

In Luke 18:9-14, there's a story about two men who go up to a mountain to pray, but only one of them actually prays.

When the Pharisee, who is the religious leader goes to the mountain to pray, he boasts about how he practices a form of asceticism that is beyond the norm. He goes on about his accomplishments, compares himself to others, and then judges the tax collector near him. The focus is not really on who God is, it is actually on what he does.

When the Tax Collector, who is seen as a sinner and a traitor, goes to the mountain to pray, he begins with the fact that he's a sinner, which means he begins with the truth about his own weakness. This man knows how fragile he is, how imperfect he is, and how in need of grace he is.

He doesn't justify, explain, avoid or perform. He just simply and vulnerably lays down his defenses before the presence of God.

And Jesus says that it is the tax collector that goes home justified before God.

You can sing, and shout, and pray, and read your Bible, and even lead a church, but without honesty and humility, you will not know the freedom that only comes from the vulnerable presence of God that is always waiting to be let in to your life.

Maybe you don't need to read your Bible more right now, because what you need is to find a safe space to be brutally honest about the hurt you are carrying.

Maybe you don't need to go to another big conference, and instead commit to find a therapist who can help you work through some of the trauma that is coming to the surface.

Maybe you don't need to go on another twenty-one day fast or commit to another six month Bible reading plan, because what you need to do in order to receive the freedom you want is to actually forgive your mother or father.

While an old friend of mine was working at a megachurch fifteen to twenty years ago, he was part of the team that was responsible for planning the up and coming staff retreat. At the beginning of this process, he wanted to leverage some of the great relationships he had to make the retreat a new and unique experience for the staff. So he reached out to a well known spiritual writer, to see if he was willing to lead the teaching element of the retreat.

The writer knew my friend was on staff at a large evangelical megachurch, so he was aware of the kind of environment he was going to be stepping into if he did it. So when my friend asked him to do it, he said he would, but only under one condition. My friend kind of smiled a little bit, getting curious about what he was going to say, then asked him what was the one condition.

Without hesitation he said, "No one is allowed to bring their Bibles."

At this point, my friend laughed a little to himself knowing he was going to have to explain all of this to the senior pastor in order to get him to sign off on everything. So through this subtle laugh, he followed up by asking why he didn't want any one bringing their Bible.

He replied, "Because evangelicals hide from God in their Bibles."

Everyone is susceptible to using religious activity as a way for us to avoid reality or hide from our feelings.

But pastors and religious leaders might be the most trained in doing this.

The insecure ego loves to disguise itself in religious activity.

It is easier to write sermons, lead church services, sing songs, strategize about mission, and do all the things pastors do, than to actually be honest with yourself and face God in unguarded intimacy.

So much religious activity keeps us busy, gives us the illusion that transformation is happening in our lives when it isn't, and actually functions as a defense mechanism that protects us from the truth of our lives. This is why we have so many busy Christian leaders who are driven, ambitious, successful, and falling apart, emotionally unhealthy, and standing at the edge of devastation.

So much religious activity is the just the ego dressed up in church clothes trying to stay busy.

There was this one leader I met while he was visiting California from a different state. He was a professor and a pastor. He was strong willed, outspoken, and extremely generous with his time.

At the same time, this man came from a culture that was very patriarchal, ambitious, and (from my perspective) placed more value on leadership and power than on self awareness and deep transformation. Being around him the little time I was, I always sensed there was some heaviness, unprocessed pain in his shadow, and some internal issues he had not worked through.

Years later, through a sermon I saw him give online at his school, I heard him talk about some weight and unprocessed pain he had been carrying, and how for the first time in a long time, he allowed himself to grieve.

There is no judgment there, but it struck me that while I was around him, the entire time he was inspiring people, planning for the next big movement, and working tirelessly to get there, he was carrying all of this weight.

He was leading others boldly, but he was not practicing the simple way of being real, honest and vulnerable with God. I wonder why its so much easier to publicly lead with strength than quietly allow yourself to be weak in front of the Spirit.

It's easier to try and spread the gospel to every part of the world than it is to allow the gospel to be spread to every part of your soul.

Healthy religion is not a way of escaping from your uncomfortable emotions, it is a way of embracing these emotions as the Spirit draws you to the other side of them. Deep spirituality never bypasses our wounds and pain, it takes us by the hand and walks us into everything that hurts, and stays with us as we are carried through by God.

Perhaps, this is why Jesus said, "Blessed are those who mourn, for they will be comforted" (Matthew 5:4). The real work of religion and spirituality is about the faith that there is always comfort through the grief, never the avoidance of grief itself.

So, for people of faith in general, and for religious leaders specifically, we always need to be listening to our life deeply enough to perceive whether or not in the midst of all of the religious activity we are engaged in, we are being led further on the path of honesty, intimacy, and union with God.

Real life in Christ is never about distracting ourselves from the depth of our life, it's about being led into the depth, through what feels like the distractions in our life.

FAITHFULNESS AND FRUSTRATION

From the first night of Imagine in our living room, I decided I was never going to count the number of people who were present. In the beginning, we made a decision to build a community that was created on substance over hype, authenticity over performance, and depth over breadth. To spend my energy counting how many people showed up on a Sunday for a worship gathering would be to betray the heart of church we wanted to grow, and to allow a metric system I did not believe in to shape the heart of the community.

Although in that first season of life in our house, there were probably fifteen to twenty people in the house on any given Sunday night.

(that's just an estimate, don't think I'm that much of a hypocrite)

There would be moments as we began, when we would be taking a deep breath and praying, where I would find myself starting to count the number of people sitting in the circle. But each time I would catch myself counting at about three, and I would stop, smile quietly inside, and return all of my attention to the people present. Each time I did that, it was like something within me would uncoil a little bit, this spaciousness would open up in my spirit, and I would hear God say, "this is what faithfulness looks like."

That is the question isn't?

Is faithfulness enough?

Whether people are ever aware of it or not, this is the question that hides underneath so many of the decisions we make in our lives.

(And by faithfulness, I simply mean doing the best you can.)

Is me preaching, guiding, and caring for these twenty people in my living room enough? Is me showing up and being as real with this group of people enough? Is me creating exactly what I want to create right now enough? Is me listening to this person's story right now enough? Is me being with my kids right now enough, even though a part of me feels like I am not accomplishing anything?

Through what we do, and the energy we carry, we are always asking, "Is faithfulness enough?" And even when we think we know the answer, our concrete lives are the only ones trustworthy enough to answer that question honestly.

Every time we work ourselves to the point of burn out, our life is saying that it's not.

Every time we try and manipulate or win people over in order to know where we stand with them, our life is saying that its not.

Every time we take time in our minds to measure whether or not our accomplishments for the day justify our existence in this universe, our life is saying it's not.

Too often, our minds want to quickly answer the question and say, "Of course I believe that faithfulness is enough," even though it is clear from our neurotic, overworked, anxious, and grasping energy that the rest of our life isn't so sure about the answer.

So when the brilliant monk Thich Nhat Hanh said, "I vow to eat, drink, and work in ways the preserve my health and well being[,]" he speaks of a life that is grounded in enough. No one who trusts that they're enough ever works in a way that compromises their health or undermines their well being.

Recently, I had a long conversation with an old classmate of mine, who is a pastor on the East Coast. Within the frustration and vulnerability of the moment, the energy pulsating within her was one of dissatisfaction and heaviness. Since my friend was doing everything she's ever dreamed of vocationally, the issue here was not what she was doing—the real issue was the frustration with how others were responding to what she was doing.

It was how many people showed up to her Sunday services. It was the struggle to not personalize the degree of change (or lack there of) people were putting on display with their life. It was the comparison of her life with the lives of other pastors who—based on cultural metrics that have nothing to do with the way and words of Jesus—seemed to be more successful than her.

It wasn't the true self's natural expression of authenticity, it was the ego's need for approval.

It wasn't the true self's unique vocation, it was the ego's need for validation.

It wasn't the true self's desire to be real, it was the ego's need for recognition.

Hidden in plain site within so many frustrated, burnt out, and overwhelmed leaders is the simple needs of the insecure ego that still want validation outside of God.

We think it could be a million different things, but it's not.

When we are stuck in that entangled knot of anger, frustration, or discouragement in our vocation, we assume it's this irreducibly complex situation that is impossible to disentangle, but it's not. Most often, during these painful moments, we are simply not satisfied with how our work is being responded to by the public, and in order to move forward, there are some expectations we've had that we need to let go of.

The only part of you that does not trust that faithfulness is enough is your ego or your false self that is still looking for value and seeking to define itself outside of the infinite outpouring of God's love.

When we are unsatisfied with the offering from our life for the world, it's often an expression of our struggle to trust the naming and validating love of God for ourself. Thomas Merton claimed that, "To say that I am made in the image of God is to say that love is the reason for my existence, for God is love. Love is my true identity. Selflessness is my true self. Love is my true character. Love is my name."

If love is your name, your life is about offering not outcomes, and you are liberated from seeking rewards from life because love has enlightened you to see the reward of life itself.

This is why whenever we ask the question, Is faithfulness enough?

At a deeper level, I think it's actually God asking us.

Every time our tired and frustrated life asks God is faithfulness enough, it is God who answers that question with the exact same question to us.

I don't know. Is it?

Is faithfulness enough? Is faithfulness enough for you?

It can feel as if there is this deep cry from within aiming itself toward the heavens pleading that our offering will be received as enough so we can finally rest and feel at ease. But God is already okay and expects no blood sacrifices, miracles, or shows from us.

God already trusts in our faithfulness, and I assume God keeps wondering why we don't.

It has been seven years since those living room circles gave birth to the community of Imagine. Which means it has been seven years of sermons,
dinners,
singing,
baptisms,
tears,
laughter,
embrace,
communion,
and expanding in the way of Jesus.

And after seven years of our communal life together in Christ, I have never counted the number of people who have showed up on a Sunday for worship. I simply refuse to allow any metrics, numbers, or systems that are born out of a corporate culture to define the value of my offering. To use any other metric outside of the authentic offering of my life for the world to define my value would be to betray the very nature of the Christ I claim to be doing this for.

So, each time I have asked God that loaded question, is faithfulness enough?

And God has responded by rightfully asking me if I believe faithfulness is enough.

Beyond the voice of my ego demanding more and the part of my ego that says I should be further along than I am, through the tears, smiles, and a deep buoyancy in my heart, I have always eventually answered yes.

SEEING THE JOURNEY AND DOING THE JOURNEY

When I drive, I listen to podcasts and stand up comedy more than I listen to music.

Although the truth is since I have a four year old and a two year old, I hardly listen to any of them.

But if someone were to do research on my listening habits, or if the algorithms were to find the connecting threads of my content, they could best be described at the point of convergence between comedy, contemplative spirituality, and profanity—which is also how some may describe my natural approach to pastoring too.

My content flows naturally between the profane and hilarious stories of stand up comedians, the reflections and views of the some of the most profound mystics alive today, and moments where I'm sure if people could see how entertained I was by what I was listening to comedically, they would be concerned for my soul.

Don't worry.

I know what I'm doing.

I have to admit that in all of my listening, there is one thing that I dislike more than anything else—when I hear a thought leader say something about spirituality that I sense they do not know for themselves.

As I'm listening, a person will say something about life and God, or share a piece of wisdom that I agree with. But then, I will immediately sense a disconnect when I hear it. In those moments, it's not that I disagree with what they are saying, it's that their interior space seems to not personally know what they are saying. I don't disagree with the content they're sharing, the content itself seems to disagree with the truth of their life.

The truth of a spiritual statement is not just about whether or not a person understands it in their mind, it's about whether or not it has awakened in their heart and unfolded through their body.

There's a difference between seeing the journey and doing the journey.

There's a difference between learning and living.
There's a difference between believing and becoming.
There are ideas.
There is incarnation.
These are not the same thing.

Haven't you ever heard someone say something deep in a conversation with others, see a person post a quote on Instagram, or watch somebody you know well share about the life changing wisdom they learned, knowing damn well they don't actually live out what they are saying.

And you find yourself sort of stunned and in disbelief, thinking, "are you really saying this shit right now with a straight face?"

Those moments are hilarious to me. It's like having a little inside joke between you and yourself.

Early one evening, we were driving home from an epic day on the North Shore here on Oahu. This moment was as perfect of an adventure-all-day-in-Hawaii moment as you can get. We spent all day at the beach, ate amazing food, saw some legendary surf spots, and now as the sun was setting over the water as we were driving into these majestic mountains, I look to my friend to the right, and he's on the phone.

Now, my friend who was visiting Hawaii, happens to be a successful writer, and as I am simultaneously in amazement at both the unmatched beauty of Hawaii and the fact that his face is focused on his screen, I cannot contain myself and I playfully go off.

"Yeah, its so great to write such powerful words about the connections between beauty and justice, and yet be unable to actually appreciate beauty when it's here. It's so powerful to write with such eloquence about the need to be present, and yet be completely unable to actually be present in this once in a lifetime moment. I guess what matters is how it all sounds when we write, right? Right!?"

Okay, first, I love this guy.

Second, I was just joking.

Kind of.

When we hear thought leaders, clergy, or spiritual teachers saying profound things about life, the truth is anybody can say these things. Which means the real questions that determines the truth of what is being said is, do you directly actualized that for yourself? Are you speaking with the awakened authority that comes from knowing this for yourself? Or is this just a clever one liner for you to share?

Seeing the path with our eyes and walking the path with our feet are not the same thing.

If you were to look at a map of surf spots on the south shore of Honolulu, you could gain a lot of information about where to surf here in town. You could learn that Ala Moana Bowls is the best left, and arguably the best wave in town. You could see that "Rennex" is the surf spot just south of Kewalos. And by looking at the map, and reading descriptions about the wave, you could know that Off The Rocks is close to the edge of Magic Island, and that Big Rights is in the middle of Ala Moana Beach Park.

Also, by exploring the maps, not only could you know some detailed information about surfing in Honolulu, you could actually teach others that same knowledge that you learned. You could learn information about the surf spots, and teach that knowledge to others without ever having visited Hawaii, getting in the water to surf, and experiencing the terrain for yourself.

But being familiar with the map is not the same as knowing the terrain.

Understanding the map can't teach you that on a good day at Bowls, you might be surfing with eighty other people. The map doesn't tell you that the surf spot "Rennex" is named that because it's right next, or "rennex" to Kewalos. And no matter how detailed the map might be, it is not the same as knowing that when you are surfing Off the Rocks, you will literally be surfing a spot with coral heads popping out of the water in front of you when you are taking off on a wave. And no map can ever make you feel what you will feel when you see just how big the rights are at Big Rights as you are anxiously paddling toward the channel to duck dive the set that is coming.

We can be familiar with the map, without ever knowing the terrain.

We can be very passionate learning about things without actually living those things.

We can build a following talking about the truth that we are currently unable to live.

This is why we have therapists who are so gifted in guiding others toward peace, who are still highly neurotic, constantly anxious, and unable to walk the path to healing they give others directions to. This is why we have yoga teachers who are so eloquent when they talk about being present, letting go, and trusting the universe, who are still addicted, co-dependent, and living in a consistent state of fear. This is why we have pastors who preach moving sermons about grace and resting in God's love, and who are still unable to access grace for themselves, and who anxiously over work themselves trying to prove their worth and win people over.

It's like we have a bunch of experts who build beautiful conceptual cathedrals for others that they rarely step foot in themselves.

Too often, we mistake the map with the terrain, learning about something and knowing it for ourselves, and communicating the content of the truth to others without experiencing the substance of that truth for ourselves.

+ + +

Jesus said, "Your eye is the lamp of your body. When your eyes are healthy, your whole body also is full of light."

Spirituality is about seeing.

Clarity gives birth to wisdom, allows for an open and creative expression of love to lead us, and empowers our imagination to be driven by that powerful question, "what if?" while the status quo remains bound to what is.

Clarity leads the way for our minds, hearts, and bodies to align themselves into a seamless and cooperative relationship called integrity.

Clarity is about seeing.

While clarity is the beginning point of transformation, it is not transformation in and of itself.

Beginning the movement from seeing the journey to doing the journey starts with clarity, but it is only completed through courage. Clarity allows you to see the path toward freedom, but only courage is able to walk that path.

The pastor can preach that sermon and give you the clarity you need to realize how essential forgiving your sister is, but only courage is able to sit still, face the anger and hurt long enough, and feel the pain deep enough to truly release and forgive.

Your yoga teacher can describe the flow of letting go and give you clarity on how foundational it is for our well being, but only courage can confront the resentment and the pain within, and hold that space in the presence of love to truly be able to let go.

Your therapist can provide the utmost clarity on how your default patterns in interpersonal relationships keep leading you to close off or push away the people who want to love you. But only courage can recognize those patterns as they arise, resist the impulse to react when they do, and allow that anxiety and discomfort to sit in your body long enough for their power to be exhausted so you can choose to trust.

Clarity is what enables you to believe, but only courage empowers you to become.

Too often, we live as if the real issue when it comes to transformation is a lack of clarity, when in reality the defining thing is the need for courage. We head back to another workshop, listen to another podcast, take some more notes, gain some more clarity and say, "Ooh, that's good."

When the truth is that if we want to actually do the journey, sometimes what we need is to sit somewhere quiet, face what is in us, or practice vulnerability with someone we trust, and have the courage to feel whatever we need to feel and say, "Wow, this hurts."

This is why Jesus says, follow me.
Not just believe in me.
Not just think correctly about me.

Not just talk about me.
But follow me.

Here we move from learning about life from Jesus, to living the life of Jesus.

The truth of what we say is determined by the depth of our own realization. Doesn't this make perfect sense? Our lives are not going to be changed because we are familiar with the map of ideas, they are going to be changed because we become familiar with the texture of the terrain the map is helping us make sense of.

Seeing the journey with clarity is interesting and exciting, and if you can teach it passionately enough, it will put you on stages in front of crowds. But simply seeing the journey will not open up the way toward the fullness of Christ. Doing the journey is quiet and humble, and while it will not further your brand at all, it will set you free.

Truth is an experience.

It is an adventure.

It is the very Spirit of God that is unfolding in the entire universe evolving in you, through you, and as your very life. Taking that mysterious and critical step from seeing the journey to doing the journey is what enlightens our eyes and enables us to see.

We always have to remember, the best translation of the word of God is not in greek and Hebrew, it is in flesh and blood.

THE MYSTIC IS DEAD

All mystics know that death is the secret to life.

Surrendering control is the only thing required to feel secure. Letting go of the need to protect ourselves is the unexpected path toward feeling safe. Releasing any expectations on life is what opens up the possibility to be content with life.

Surrendering, letting go, and releasing are all forms of dying.

Dying is what makes living possible.

The mystic is simply the one who knows God intimately. They are also the one who embraces death frequently. Which is why it would be most accurate to say the mystic knows God so intimately because they embrace death so frequently.

The denial of death is the denial of God, the denial of grace, and the denial of life. Because whenever you consciously embrace death, let go, or trust, the Spirit that "holds all things together," (Col. 1:17) holds you together.

Which means, the more I resist death, the more I miss out on life.

Even though the lives and experiences of the rare and true mystics are seen with a modern and romantic lens, the journey of a real mystic is anything but romantic.

Why is that? Well…

the mystic is the one who voluntarily chooses to die.

Of course, the mystics are the seers who leave silence with poetry, live in light so unpretentiously that their glow is the only reward that matters to them. The mystics are the ones who fuse with God so organically that it's hard to tell the difference in the the slight distinction between their spirit and Spirit itself.

But also, they are the ones who quietly bear the suffering of the world in their hearts, intensely wrestle with God and imperfection on behalf of all humanity, and do not have the luxury of compartmentalization, denial, or avoidance.

I know.
I'm being dramatic again!
But it's true.

To be a mystic is to intentionally face within what most people only face if life and suffering force them to. It is common for people to only begin to wake up to what in them needs to die when they have lost something, experienced tragedy, or had the things that mean the most to them taken away. And when they have been pushed to the edge of their own inner resources and feel things falling apart, that is when people allow themselves to start looking within at what is really getting in the way.

Or, what it is that needs to die.

The mystic does not have the luxury of avoiding what lurks in the shadow of their lives, and they do not wait until they are forced by circumstantial suffering to begin confronting their darkness. For them, the ego humiliating inward journey that for most people is a forced timeout they go on once a year, is actually a part of their daily routine.

The mystic calmly walks to the edges of their life, recognizes the boundaries, names the wounds, sits with the illusions, and eventually surrenders, feels, releases, and lets go of anything that is getting in the way of the natural movement toward freedom.

The mystic freely lets go of the things most people have to be forced to.

At seventeen and eighteen years old, my life was going very well. I was getting a good amount of public attention for sports and had the chance to play in college, I was becoming more and more recognized as a rapper, (that's a long story), I always had money from selling weed, I was known in the party scene, and was completely aware that I had everything all of my friends and peers wanted.

My life was working great.

And I decided to walk away from it all. (I know, I mentioned this before.)

I didn't walk away because my life wasn't working, I walked away because I knew I wasn't free, and I knew what I had wasn't real.

I had attention from sports and music, but I knew that kind of attention just gave me a false sense of validation that didn't actually make feel whole.

I had all kinds of people who wanted to be around me because of what I did, but I knew that they didn't actually know me or value me for who I was.

I accepted that my entire life was being driven by my insecure ego that was constantly seeking attention, doing everything for validation, and was living my life to achieve a level of status that I no longer believed in.

Most people only move on when they hit bottom, mystics can walk away when they're at the top.

I could see at eighteen that striving, grasping, and achieving a name from others wasn't the way. I also began to trust that dying, letting go, and receiving a name from God was the only way. I never fought the surrendering I was beginning, I wasn't angry about letting go of what I was doing, and I wasn't resisting the dying to my ego self—no matter how successful it was—because I knew that the only things that were dying were things getting in the way of my future.

The only things we ever let go of are things get in the way of our freedom.

The only parts of ourself we die to are the parts that are not truly us.

The only ego needs we surrender are the ones that we don't actually need to experience joy.

When speaking about death and transformation, the great mystic Thomas Merton said, "It means to be nailed to the cross with

Christ, so that the ego-self is no longer the principle of our deepest actions, which now proceed from Christ living in us."

Dying to and transcending the ego is the first major step in a real journey of transformation. This is where you are not just aware of the interworking of your ego (that's self awareness), but when you actually de-center the ego as the primary center from which you live your life (that is transformation).

This is why on the front of a famous monastery, the doorpost says "If you die before you die, then when you die, you won't die."

This is why Richard Rohr says that, "all great spirituality is about letting go."

This why St. Gregory of Nyssa said, "No one gets as much of God as those who are thoroughly dead."

This is why Ken Wilber wrote, "Every form of meditation is basically a way to transcend the ego, or die to the ego."

This is why Ilia Delio wrote, "To say "I will not die" is to die. To be willing to die by surrendering to the freedom of the Spirit is to live forever."

This is why the Apostle Paul said, "it is no longer I who live, but Christ who lives in me (Galatians 2:20).

This is why Jesus said, "Whoever wants to be my disciple must deny themselves and take up their cross and follow me (Mark 8:34).

What every great mystic, including Jesus, is saying is that dying to the ego and all of its needs, and discovering your true self is nothing but taking off an old outfit that you wore for a while, does not fit you any more, and was never meant to be worn forever.

We are all invited to do this. I just happened to trust it and embrace early in life.

The mystic knows life is about trusting death.

The entire structure and forward movement of the cosmos is held together by the dynamic of transcending and including, and the power in the biblical narrative emerges through a story of death and resurrection.

The transformation of consciousness, the evolution of culture, the expansion of the universe, and the story of Jesus are all saying in their own unique way, trust the death because it always leads to more life.

I walked away from everything I knew at eighteen and embraced that dark night of the soul because I trusted the death of what I knew.

I let go of the life of attention and applause, and embraced a life of invisibility for ten years, because I trusted the death of those old ego needs.

As a pastor, I can allow our church to be exactly where it is without being governed by frustration or anxiety because I consistently trust the death of wherever I think she's supposed to be.

Through all of the hurt, betrayal, and pain I have received from life, I have never shut down my heart and live with no resentment or bitterness, because each time I have been hurt, I have trusted the death that was needed to move forward. This is why mystics evolve so quickly, change so fast, and grow so much—every time they are confronted with any kind of barrier, hurt, or ego boundary, they can move into acceptance, letting go, and embrace the death of the moment naturally.

The mystic always knows that refusing to surrender is denying the natural movement of the Spirit.

At eighteen, everything that brought me a false sense of security, I let go of. Everything that had given me a sense of value outside of being known by the Spirit I allowed to die. Everything that had made me feel like me, I surrendered because I trusted that through the Spirit, something even more real would be born in its place.

Like any other practice, the more you do something, the better you get at it, and the easier it becomes. For the mystic, letting go, trusting each death, and crossing each and every threshold into the unknown is as natural of a movement as anything else.

We've been to the edge of our own boundaries and crossed over the lines that we thought defined our self so many times, that what is paralyzing for so many has become practical for us. We've died to so many heart breaking illusions, we've let go of so many precious expectations, there's no longer the same kind of resistance to the process the ego once lived with.

We refuse to resist the very thing that reveals who we are, and we've learned to trust that death always leads to resurrection.

The mystics know for themselves that on the other side of death is

Always resurrection.
Always expansion.
Always more spacious.
Always more freedom.
Always more grace.
Always more love.
Always more life.
Always more God.
Always more you.

We've learned that death doesn't change anything essential. We know that each death that we think has the potential to destroy who we are, carries the power to help us discover who we are.

Every illusion that we've relinquished gives birth to more clarity about what life truly is, and gives us more freedom to love it, embrace it, and accept it.

Every wound we have consciously experienced the pain of in the presence of God has led us to experience more wholeness.

Every time we surrendered the way we thought things were supposed to be, and accepted the way things are, a space has opened up that has given the Spirit the freedom to create what will be. Which is always beyond everything we tried to create in the first place.

Every time we recognized the drives and desires of our ego, dis-identified with them, and died to the need to have them fulfilled—no matter who much success they have brought us—God has always made us more authentic and more free.

+ + +

This is why mystics are dangerous.

We can not be bought by any institution. We do not withhold ourselves due to the fear of consequences because we know any negative consequences take nothing away from who we are at our essential center. We can not be shamed, manipulated, and controlled because we know that any mistake we make takes nothing away from our primary identity of love.

We do not follow the same rules as the dominant culture because we are no longer playing the ego games that hold that culture together.

Mystics do not fear vulnerability.

Vulnerability comes from the Latin 'vulnus" which means wounds. So, to be vulnerable is to be a person who can be wounded, or to be one who is woundable. We fear vulnerability because we are scared to get hurt, to be rejected, to be humiliated, to be shamed, to be abandoned, to be exposed, to be judged, or to experience whatever form of wound we fear the most.

We're scared of vulnerability because we fear being wounded, and we fear being wounded so much because—consciously or unconsciously—we believe there are certain hurts we might feel that we will not be able to handle or ever recover from.

The mystic knows this is not true.

While in my twenties and living in Orange County, a pastor I knew from a church in a different state asked a few younger people who he knew to come and preach one summer. Since I was trying to take steps forward into my sense of calling to teach and preach, this was a truly exciting opportunity for me at the time.

When Summer came around, I discovered that the other young men he invited got a chance to preach, and the pastor had forgotten to get back to me. And when I found out I was deeply hurt.

I remember being outside when I first realized what happened. My eyes welled up with tears, and I felt frustrated and discouraged because I felt like I was doing what I could to take small steps toward my future with God, and still being disappointed.

After a couple years after starting our church, my wife and I, and a group friends who are all creatives, started a creative community in our neighborhood. We had this great start, we had some of the most talented and exciting creatives in Hawaii who were a part of it, and it was going as well as it could. But after some time, I realized with my responsibilities with Imagine and a new kid, I did not have the time and energy to sustain or develop it.

So, after one last event, I decided to just end it.

I have had countless things like this happen in my life. I've disappointed people who I care about, I have been the guy who forgot to include someone and ended up hurting them, I've had the people I love the most in life be the ones who have caused me the most pain, I've ended creative initiatives I have started.

I've had virtually every one of my greatest fears in life come true. And as you sit in the weight of your greatest fears coming true with the Spirit, not only do you survive it, but you expand, grow, and become more you each time

Why would I be controlled forever by a fear of vulnerability when anything that can happen to me when I am vulnerable does not have the power to threaten or take away anything from who I am?

The mystic has already discovered that everything you fear that could possibly happen when you are vulnerable is not the end. We have already experienced tragedy, already felt pain, come face to face with those powerful fears, and felt them all the way through.

We have died to the illusion that peace is going to come by trying to create a world where these things are not possible.

The mystic is the one who has grieved, wept, let go, felt, accepted, and absorbed more pain than most people can even fathom, and come out the other side more free than most people can even imagine.

We have come to know that the resurrection does not does not guard us from pain, it guides us through pain. That the path of Christ does not mean there are no losses, it means there is always new life. And that creative freedom does not mean you're not going to fail, it means the failure is not final.

We know the resurrection does not protect us from suffering, it sustains us though suffering. And we've discovered that resurrection does not deny death, it defeats it.

In 2013, I was flying back to Hawaii from Miami, and had a layover in Houston. Somebody who I had never met before got my number and called me up to talk about a presentation they were giving at some conference that was coming up.

They were asking for guidance on something they were working on, and I told them I had about twenty minutes before I was hopping on my next flight. So, for the next twenty minutes as we chatted about his topic, I listened and shared as I was kind of walking around the airport and pacing. I was walking back and forth, zig zagging between gates, and in this constant state of motion.

And right near the end of the conversation, the most unexpected and fascinating thing happened to me.

A white, middle aged man, who was dressed for a meeting in a board room (or at least what I assume people wear in board rooms) tapped me on the shoulder. And as I told my conversation partner on the phone to hold on for a second, I looked up and the man said to me, without any hesitation and looking me straight in the eyes,

"You have nothing to offer this world."

And then he walked away.

Let that moment sink in.

In one short, but powerful sentence, he essentially obliterated the idea that my existence was worth anything in this universe. He essentially said I have nothing to contribute, which most people receive as a challenge to their fundamental value as a human being. I am very aware that this would shock, hurt, anger, embarrass, humiliate, or offend people pretty naturally.

I also remember the first thought I had when he said that, "What an interesting thing for one human to say to another."

So, I ended the phone conversation, went back to my wife, told her what happened, kind of just laughed and marveled at the strange occurrence it was, and moved on. No lasting anger, no ongoing offense, no replaying and rehearsing of the conversation in my head, just another flight home.

Why would it bother me?

You can't offend something that is already dead.

OUTRO

I was recently on the phone with my best friend Livvy, and I was explaining to him what it was like to sit down and eat ice cream with my two kids, Mikayla and True. At this time, the kids were one and three.

I gave him a minute by minute description of what was happening as I was walking through this grocery store. I explained how my kids were reaching for fruit, trying to grab toys, stopping to say hi to the lobsters in the tanks, and jumping up to grip the counter as I ordered their ice cream. Which didn't even cover the walk back through the market, before we got to the little grassy area out side of H-Mart.

Much to my friend's shock and disbelief, I then painted the picture of what it was like to sit down with both of them, and split the two scoops of ice cream into one cup. I told him how my son was climbing on me and aggressively asking me for his ice cream through his cute little gibberish, as my daughter waited for her own personal cup of unicorn poop ice cream.

That was the actual flavor.

I then told him how, as my son sat on my lap, he would make a loud and defiant noise whenever I tried to feed him. And how instead of allowing his dad to feed him, he began shoving his face so close to the cup that his long hair is completely enveloping the cup.

And of course, while this was happening, my sweet and generous daughter keeps wanting to give me a bite of her yummy unicorn poop ice cream. But since the ice cream is melting, every time she reaches to do it, she drips entire bites onto my shoes and my shorts.

While this is happening as a parent, you can feel the triggers of frustration start to emerge in a visceral way. You can feel your expectations on how this should go, or your ideal version of this moment crashing into the reality of what is happening, and it becomes so easy to be frustrated, angry, or overwhelmed.

After describing the insanity of that ten minute scene to my friend, through the kind of sacred laughter that leaves your cheeks hurting in the end, I told my friend that in that moment that I said to myself,

"The only way to enjoy this is to let it be the uncontrollable mess that it is."

And if you respond by asking, "Do you mean that moment with your kids or life as a whole?"

The answer is yes.

The magic is always in the mess.

+ + +

For the mystic,

It's the laughter after the letting go.
It's the silliness after the surrender.
It's the freedom after the fighting.

It's the hilariousness after the heaviness.
It's the trust after the trauma.
It's the ability to relax after wrestling with reality.

The secret always lies within the resurrection after the death,
and the freedom that comes from surrendering to the God who
doesn't protect us from everything, but sustains us through
anything. For the mystic, it is always the joy that comes from the
wild embrace that everything is finite, fragile, and deconstructible,
except for the indestructible force of love itself.

The mystic takes life almost uncomfortably seriously, and yet not
seriously at all. We laugh in the face of death because we have
wept through thousands of our own funerals along the way. We
are always tiptoeing along the edge of heresy, dancing on top
of the tables of orthodoxy, and laughing at the walls insecure
religious people keep building. We keep performing all of the
religious rituals with a subtle smile and a wink, knowing that
nobody needs anyone to open the doors to the house they're
already in. While at the same time being more than happy to give
them a key.

BOOKS REFERENCED

Cynthia Bourgeault, *Wisdom Jesus: Transforming Heart and Mind—A New Perspective on Christ And His Message* (Boston, MA: Shambhala, 2008)

Cynthia Bourgeault, *The Heart of Centering Prayer: Nondual Christianity in Theory and Practice* (Boston, MA: Shambhala, 2016)

Walter Brueggemann, *Hopeful Imagination: Prophetic Voices in Exile* (Philadelphia, PA: Fortress Press, 1986)

Ilia Delio, *Making All Things New: Catholicity, Cosmology, Consciousness* (Maryknoll. NY: Or-bis, 2015)

Meister Eckhart, *Treatises and Sermons of Meister Eckhart* (New York, NY: Harper & Bros, 1958)

Hafiz, Daniel Ladinsky, *I Heard God Laughing: Poems of Hope and Joy* (New York, NY: Pen-guin Books, 2006)

Thich Nhat Hanh, *Living Buddha, Living Christ* (New York, NY: Riverhead Books, 1995)

Abraham Joshua Heschel, *The Sabbath* (New York, NY. Farrar, Strauss, Giroux, 1951)

Shane Hipps, *Selling Water by the River: A Book about the Life Jesus Promised and the Religion That Gets in the Way* (New York, NY: Jericho Books, 2012)

Gary Laderman, *Sacred Matters: Celebrity Worship, Sexual Ecstasies, The Living Dead and Other Signs of Religious Life in the United States* (New York, NY: The New Press, 2009)

Daniel Ladinsky, *Love Poems from God: Twelve Sacred Voices from the East and West* (London, UK: Penguin Books, 2002)

Steve McIntosh, *The Presence of the Infinite: The Spiritual Experience of Beauty, Truth, and Goodness* (Wheaton, IL: Quest Books, 2015)

Thomas Merton, Kathleen Deignan, *A Book of Hours* (Notre Dame, IN: Sorin Books, 2007)

Thomas Merton, *New Seeds of Contemplation* (New York, NY: New Directions, 1961)

Thomas Merton, *No Man is an Island* (New York, NY: HarperOne, 2002

Thomas Merton, *Springs of Contemplation: A Retreat At The Abbey of Gethsemane* (New York, NY: Farrar, Strauss, Giroux, 1992)

Thomas Merton, *Zen and the Birds of Appetite* (New York, NY: New Directions, 1968)

John Phillip Newell, *The Re-Birthing of God: Christianity's Struggle for New Beginnings* (Wood-stock, VT: Christian Journeys, 2014)

Richard Rohr, *The Divine Dance: The Trinity and Your Transformation* (New Kensington, PA: Whitaker House, 2016)

Richard Rohr, *Immortal Diamond: The Search For Our True Self* (San Francisco, CA: Jossey-Bass, 2013)

Richard Rohr, *The Naked Now: Learning To See As The Mystics See* (New York, NY: The Crossroad Publishing Company, 2009)

Rumi, If you can find the origins of Rumi's beautiful words, well done.

Huston Smith, *Tales of Wonder: Adventures Chasing the Divine, an Autobiography* (New York, NY: HarperOne, 2009)

Paul R. Smith, *Integral Christianity: The Spirit's Call to Evolve* (St. Paul, MI: Paragon House, 2011)

Mirabai Starr, *Wild Mercy: Living the Fierce and Tender Wisdom of the Women Mystics* (Boul-der, CO: Sounds True, 2019)

Alan Watts, *The Joyous Cosmology, Adventures in the Chemistry of Consciousness* (Novato, CA: New World Library, 2013)

Ken Wilber, "Death, Rebirth, and Meditation" in G. Doore, ed., *What Survives?: Contemporary Ex-ploration of Life After Death*, Tarcher, 1990, pp. 176-91

Ken Wilber, *The Simple Feeling of Being: Embracing Your True Nature* (Boston, MA: Shambha-la, 2004)

Ken Wilber, *The Religion of Tomorrow: A Vision for the Future of the Great Traditions—More Inclusive, More Comprehensive, More Complete* (Boulder, CO: Shambhala, 2017)

Ken Wilber, *One Taste: Daily Reflections on Integral Spirituality* (Boston, MA: Shambhala, 2000)

https://www.patheos.com/blogs/rogereolson/2019/10/some-thoughts-about-celebrities-who-become-christians-and-then/

For more information about Kevin Sweeney
or to contact him for speaking engagements,
connect with him on Instagram @kevinsweeney1

Many voices. One message.

Quoir is a boutique publisher
with a singular message: Christ is all.
Venture beyond your boundaries to discover Christ
in ways you never thought possible.

For more information, please visit
www.quoir.com

9 781957 007144